D0431318

I Can't Believe They Asked Me That!

By Ron and Caryl Krannich

CAREER AND BUSINESS BOOKS
101 Secrets of Highly Effective Speakers
201 Dynamite Job Search Letters
The $100,000+ Entrepreneur
America's Top 100 Jobs for People Without a Four-Year Degree
America's Top Jobs for People Re-Entering the Workforce
America's Top Internet Job Sites
Best Jobs for the 21st Century
Best Resumes and Letters for Ex-Offenders
Blue Collar Resume and Job Hunting Guide
Change Your Job, Change Your Life
The Complete Guide to Public Employment
The Directory of Federal Jobs and Employers
Discover the Best Jobs for You!
Dynamite Salary Negotiations
Dynamite Tele-Search
The Educator's Guide to Alternative Jobs and Careers
The Ex-Offender's Job Hunting Guide
The Ex-Offender's Quick Job Hunting Guide
Find a Federal Job Fast!
From Air Force Blue to Corporate Gray
From Army Green to Corporate Gray
From Navy Blue to Corporate Gray
Get a Raise in 7 Days
High Impact Resumes and Letters
I Can't Believe They Asked Me That!
I Want to Do Something Else, But I'm Not Sure What It Is
Interview for Success
The Job Hunting Guide: Transitioning From College to Career
Job Hunting Tips for People With Hot and Not-So-Hot Backgrounds
Job Interview Tips for People With Not-So-Hot Backgrounds
Jobs and Careers With Nonprofit Organizations
Military Transition to Civilian Success
Military Resumes and Cover Letters
Nail the Cover Letter!
Nail the Job Interview!
Nail the Resume!
No One Will Hire Me!
Overcoming Barriers to Employment
Overcoming 101 More Barriers to Employment
Re-Careering in Turbulent Times
Savvy Interviewing
The Savvy Networker
The Savvy Resume Writer
Win the Interview, Win the Job

TRAVEL AND INTERNATIONAL BOOKS
Best Resumes and CVs for International Jobs
The Complete Guide to International Jobs and Careers
The Directory of Websites for International Jobs
International Jobs Directory
Jobs for Travel Lovers
Shopping in Exotic Places
Shopping the Exotic South Pacific
Travel Planning On the Internet
Treasures and Pleasures of Australia
Treasures and Pleasures of Bermuda
Treasures and Pleasures of China
Treasures and Pleasures of Egypt
Treasures and Pleasures of Hong Kong
Treasures and Pleasures of India
Treasures and Pleasures of Indonesia
Treasures and Pleasures of Italy
Treasures and Pleasures of Mexico
Treasures and Pleasures of Paris
Treasures and Pleasures of Rio and São Paulo
Treasures and Pleasures of Santa Fe, Taos, and Albuquerque
Treasures and Pleasures of Singapore
Treasures and Pleasures of South America
Treasures and Pleasures of Southern Africa
Treasures and Pleasures of Thailand and Myanmar
Treasures and Pleasures of Turkey
Treasures and Pleasures of Vietnam and Cambodia

I Can't Believe They Asked Me That!

110 Tips and Techniques to Quickly Prepare for a Tough Job Interview

Ron and Caryl Krannich, Ph.Ds

IMPACT PUBLICATIONS
Manassas Park, VA

It Can't Believe They Asked Me That!

ISBN: 978-1-57023-256-5 (13-digit), 1-57023-256-3 (10-digit)

Library of Congress: 2006932516

Publisher: For information on Impact Publications, including current and forthcoming publications, authors, press kits, online bookstore, and submission requirements, visit the left navigation bar on the front page of our main company website: www.impactpublications.com.

Publicity/Rights: For information on publicity, author interviews, and subsidiary rights, contact the Media Relations Department: Tel. 703-361-7300, Fax 703-335-9486, or email: query@impactpublications.com.

Sales/Distribution: All bookstore sales are handled through Impact's trade distributor: National Book Network, 15200 NBN Way, Blue Ridge Summit, PA 17214, Tel. 1-800-462-6420. All special sales and distribution inquiries should be directed to the publisher: Sales Department, IMPACT PUBLICATIONS, 9104 Manassas Drive, Suite N, Manassas Park, VA 20111-5211, Tel. 703-361-7300, Fax 703-335-9486, or email: query@impactpublications.com.

Contents

Index to Tips

CHAPTER 5
You Mean There's More Than One?

CHAPTER 6
Actions Speak Louder Than Words
Making Good First Impressions

CHAPTER 7
Anticipate Questions and Tell Your Story

CHAPTER 8
Ask Thoughtful Questions

CHAPTER 9
Remember to Close and Follow Up

CHAPTER 10
Get the Offer, Then Talk Money to Power

Preface

THE JOB INTERVIEW IS THE single most important step to getting a job offer. Everything you have done thus far in your job search – conducting research, writing resumes and letters, submitting applications, and networking – should have prepared you for the job interview.

A Disconnect

All too often, however, there's a big disconnect somewhere along the way to the interview site. Indeed, many candidates, who ostensibly prepared for this important encounter, return from a job interview lamenting, *"I can't believe they asked me that!"* Instead of being well prepared for the interview, they made numerous mistakes that could have been avoided had they simply prepared well for all types of interviews as well as different phases of the job interview.

Approaches and Trends

This book is designed to quickly prepare you for the job interview by offering 110 tips for interview success. It's not about how to provide clever answers to tricky interview questions, although we do address this issue and offer lists of anticipated questions. While recognizing the importance of preparing for anticipated questions, we purposefully avoided the traditional question/answer (Q&A) approach to the subject for four reasons:

1. **Q&A approaches offer practice questions and answers that tend to promote bad interview preparation habits** – memorization and canned answers that can turn off potential employers who are looking for evidence of authenticity, intelligence, capacity to learn, and the ability to solve problems.

2. **Q&A approaches tend to focus on traditional interview questions** which are increasingly taking a back seat to behavioral and situational interview questions. Employers continue to use more sophisticated and scientific approaches to interviewing that test the ability of candidates to think on their feet and/or deal with issues related to the job. They approach the interview as an **impromptu test** or test drive – get candidates to answer questions for which they cannot prepare as well as solve problems related to the position. More and more employers look for key **competencies** in candidates – rather than clever answers to interview questions – that relate specifically to the job.

3. **Q&A approaches tend to focus almost exclusively on the verbal interchange between the interviewee and the interviewer.** But the job interview is much more complex, especially when we realize that more than 50 percent of the job interview is nonverbal. Accordingly, candidates need to better understand and develop their nonverbal communication, which may or may not send positive messages to employers.

4. **Q&A approaches neglect other aspects of the job interview, which job seekers should prepare for in addition to answering and asking questions.** By concentrating solely on questions and answers, job seekers are ill-prepared for many other things that happen during the job interview, such as engaging in small talk, socializing at lunch or dinner, or making a presentation.

Our approach to this subject focuses on the whole interview process – from the moment you get the invitation to interview to when you are offered the job and negotiate a compensation package. Throughout this process, you need to deal with both the verbal and nonverbal aspects of the interview. Central to this process are your **attitudes** and **strategies** for success. For in the end, employers want to hire individuals who are both competent and likable. You can best communicate these important qualities by following the many tips outlined in this book.

Tell Your Unique Story

We wish you well as you prepare for the interview. Whatever you do, take the job interview very seriously. Prepare, prepare, and prepare by first developing winning attitudes and strategies for success. Become familiar with various interview questions you need to both answer and ask, but be very careful in trying to memorize answers, recite 30-second sound bites and pitches, or play the role of the perfect interviewee – behaviors that may make you sound coached, inauthentic, and suspect. Employers want to meet the **real** you – understand what you have done, can do, and will do for them in the future. It's your **pattern of accomplishments** that most interest them.

In the end, you have a compelling **story** to tell prospective employers who are very receptive to good storytellers. Your story should include employer-centered examples, illustrations, descriptions, statistics, comparisons, and testimonials that relate to your accomplishments. When you tell your story in this manner, you will most likely grab the attention of employers who, in turn, will want to quickly hire you.

The 110 interview tips revealed in this book will help you better prepare for and handle each stage of the job interview. If you put our tips into practice, you'll no longer join the ranks of surprised job seekers who return from a job interview lamenting, *"I can't believe they asked me that!"* Instead, confident of having made a good impression, you'll probably leave the interview with the employer saying, *"I can't believe we found such a fine candidate. Let's hire!"*

Ron and Caryl

1

Congratulations! Now What?

YOU GOT THE INTERVIEW. That's great! Your resumes, applications, letters, e-mails, and telephone calls finally paid off. So what are you planning to do next? Celebrate your new job? Tell everyone at work that you'll soon be leaving? Start rearranging your life in anticipation of a big raise? Buy that new car? Take that long-deserved vacation? Tell your boss that you are quitting?

But wait! Don't start making such **mental moves** about your future before you nail the job interview. While you should be upbeat, positive, and optimistic about your future, this is not the time to engage in wishful thinking or make decisions based upon **illusions**. An invitation to a job interview is not a job offer or a new job. It's only an **invitation** to meet with a prospective employer who may have arranged similar interviews with several other equally excited candidates. While your chances of getting the job are better than before, they still may not be good.

Let's not start making unrealistic plans or talk too much at work about your next job. You'll be embarrassed if you don't get the job. You may even lose your job if your boss decides to replace you in anticipation of your impending departure. Most important of all, you may become unhappy and depressed if you don't get the job offer. It's time to take a serious look at the whole job interviewing process in order to best position yourself for performing well in the job interview.

Do First Things First

An invitation to a job interview should immediately result in one thing – serious **preparation** for the interview. While you may momentarily feel good for having made this initial cut, you'll feel much better if you thoroughly prepare for the job interview. What do you know about this employer? Will you be asked to take any pre- or post-interview tests relating to your skills, attitudes, and personality? Who will interview you? Is it someone in human resources or a hiring manager? What kind of interview are you likely to encounter? Will it be just you and the interviewer or will you meet with several people? How many interviews do most candidates go through with this employer before being offered a job? How long will it take you to get to the interview site? How should you dress? What should you take with you? These are just a few of the many questions you need to address **before** meeting the interviewer and opening your mouth!

> *You need to thoroughly prepare for each stage of the interview – from the moment you walk in the door to the day you receive the job offer or a rejection.*

Once you're at the interview site, how many people are you likely to meet? How should you greet the interviewer(s)? Where do you sit? What kind of small talk would be appropriate for getting this meeting under-way? What questions are you prepared to answer? Do you know what kinds of answers most impress interviewers? What, for example, would you say if the interviewer asks you these questions or makes these comments?

- *Tell me about yourself.*
- *Why did you leave your last two jobs?*
- *What are your career plans over the next five years?*
- *What are some of your weaknesses?*
- *What are your salary expectations?*
- *Tell me about a time you disagreed with your boss.*
- *Give me an example of one of the most difficult decisions you've made in the past two years.*
- *Describe a time when you had to make a quick decision without much information.*

- *If I contacted your previous employer and asked about your performance, what might she say about your work?*
- *What are your salary requirements?*
- *Why should we hire you?*
- *Do you have any questions?*

Can you give examples of your major accomplishments? Do you have several questions you want to ask the interviewer? Do you have a list of references to give to the interviewer? Can you pass a background check with flying colors?

But you're still not done with this process. How will you close the interview? What can you do **after** you leave the interview site to influence the hiring decision? Are there certain things you can do in the post-interview stage to give you an advantage over the competition?

As you will quickly discover, there is no substitute for good interview preparation. While you may not be able to totally prepare for certain types of interviews (behavioral and situational) or tests (personality), you can at least anticipate encountering the unexpected and prepare well for those aspects of the job interview that are within your control.

Prepare to Tell Your Unique Story

Getting a job is serious business. Accordingly, treat it like a $100,000 to $1 million prize – the amount of additional income this job may generate in the coming years. Get over that momentary *"I got the interview!"* euphoria and concentrate on managing the interview to your advantage.

> *You have a unique and memorable story to tell. It's your story of work-related accomplishments employers want to hear.*

Always remember that you have an important **story** to tell employers. It's not about your personal history. Indeed, it should be a very compelling **story about your work-related accomplishments** that clearly communicates to the interviewer that you are a perfect fit for the job. It's a story that makes you unique, predictable, and memorable. Without this story, you merely become another nervous interviewee who tries to answer numerous questions with good, acceptable, and not-so-good answers. You'll leave the interview wondering how well you did and what things you forgot to say or could have said better. Worst of all, the interviewer may not remember much about you!

Interviews are all about making **good first impressions**. Within 30 to 60 minutes, you need to impress upon a stranger that a company should invest thousands of dollars in you, because you are the right person for the job. That's not much time to answer and ask many questions. Therefore, you need to make yourself instantly **memorable** with impressive stories about your accomplishments.

Focused story-tellers have a distinct advantage in the job interview. They provide **supports** in the form of examples, illustrations, and statistics about their past performance – the most important keys to effective communication. These stories become the basis for evaluating your suitability for the job.

It's Really Not About Winning

If you approach the job interview as a game involving winners and losers, you'll miss out on some of the most important outcomes of this encounter

> *A job interview is best approached as an exchange of information for deciding whether or not you will be a good "fit" for the job.*

and you may be preparing yourself for failure. Indeed, a job interview is best approached as an **exchange of information** in which both parties are trying to decide whether or not there is a good "fit" between you and the position. While you should be on your best behavior, anticipating questions and preparing thoughtful answers to tell your story and impress interviewers, above all you want to acquire more information about the employer and job in order to determine if it's best for you. Regardless of the salary and benefits offered, do you really want to invest your time and effort in this job? Is this something you will enjoy doing and will it lead to career advancement?

Preparing for Your Next Job

This book is all about quickly preparing for your next job by focusing on key elements in the interview process. Consider this likely scenario. You get a telephone call from a prospective employer who asks you a few screening questions and then invites you to a formal job interview which will take place within 24 to 48 hours. That's not much time to prepare for what may become one of the most important meetings of your life! What will you do during the next eight to 36 hours? Do you know what questions you are likely to be asked and what responses most impress interviewers? Or will you be like many candidates who leave the interview somewhat bewildered – I can't believe they asked me that! Above all, you don't want to be surprised or thrown off base with questions or experiences you are not prepared to deal with.

The interview is much more than just answering questions. It's also about managing your image from head to toe as well as impressing upon the interviewer, through both verbal and nonverbal communication, that you are the right person for the job.

The following pages will help you quickly prepare for the job interview by anticipating a variety of questions interviewers are likely to ask of you. We outline strategies on how to best respond to those questions with thoughtful and focused answers that tell your story.

But before examining those questions and answers, let's examine some of the many interviewing errors job seekers make. In so doing, you'll begin seeing the nature of the job interview from the perspective of interviewers and hiring managers.

2

Interview Mistakes Job Seekers Make
Red Flags You Should Avoid

L ET'S PUT THIS WHOLE job interview process in perspective by examining frequent interview mistakes job seekers make. Not surprisingly, job seekers make numerous interview errors, many of which employers think are "unbelievable," such as showing up late for the interview!

Like resume and letter errors, interview sins can quickly knock you out of the competition. They are **red flags** indicating you have "issues" that the employer does not wish to inherit. Unlike many other job search mistakes, interview errors tend to be both **unforgettable and unforgiving**. After all, this is the time when first impressions count the most. Make a bad first impression and the remaining minutes of your interview will be downhill and the door will permanently close behind you as you leave the interview.

Positive and Negative Goals of Employers

Employers have both positive and negative goals in mind. On the positive side, they want to hire someone who can do the job and add value or benefits to their organization. On the negative side, they are always looking for clues, or red flags, that tell them why they should **not** hire you. After all, they have made hiring mistakes before. For example, you may be another stranger who makes inflated claims about your competence, taking credit for others' accomplishments, in the hope of getting a job offer. Or perhaps you know little about the company (couldn't even find time to visit their website!), you ask about salary and benefits early in the job interview, or you fail to ask thoughtful questions – behaviors that usually indicate that a candidate is not really interested in the work and thus not a good "fit" for the organization. And if you are too social and talk too much, you may be perceived as a potentially irritating hire. Who wants to listen to you talk all day long?

It's not until you start performing on the job that the employer gets to see the "real you" and discover your attitudes and patterns of behavior. In the meantime, the employer needs to be on his or her guard looking for evidence that you may be the wrong person for the job. Make a mistake during the job interview and you may be instantly eliminated from further consideration. Therefore, you must be on your very best behavior and avoid the many common mistakes interviewers report that interviewees often make in face-to-face interviews.

40 Killer Interview Mistakes

Whatever you do, try to avoid making any of the following interview errors. Committing one of these mistakes can instantly knock you out of the competition:

1. **Arrives late to the interview.** First impressions really do count and they are remembered for a long time. Arrive late and you've made one of the worst impressions possible! Indeed, regardless of what you say or do during the interview, you may never recover from this initial mistake. Employers wonder *"Will you also come to work late?"* You may think this doesn't happen often. Think again. Some employers report that nearly 50 percent of their candidates arrive late for the interview. Such candidates offer all kinds of excuses – from legitimate to inexcusable: overslept, ran out of gas, car broke down, illness in the family, got lost, involved in an accident, roads flooded, Mapquest gave inaccurate directions, navigation system failed.

And here's the real killer excuse – *"I got lost because your directions weren't very clear."*

2. **Makes a bad impression in the waiting area.** Treats receptionists and secretaries as inferiors – individuals who may have important input into the hiring process when later asked by the interviewer or hiring manager *"What was your impression of this candidate?"* Caught reading frivolous materials – *People Magazine* – in the waiting area when company reports and related literature were readily available. Makes calls on cell phone, listens to iPod, checks e-mail, and chews gum. Asks stupid questions and/or engages in embarrassing small talk.

  Remember, this is an important time to look like a serious candidate to others who may see you and speak with you in the reception area. Don't make the mistake of believing that your interview begins once you meet the interviewer. It begins the moment you arrive at the interview site, which may be 15 minutes before the face-to-face interview session begins.

3. **Offers poor and unacceptable excuses for behavior.** Excuses are usually red flags indicating that a person is unwilling to take responsibility and do the work. Here are some excuses often heard during job interviews:

  - *I forgot.*
  - *It wasn't my fault.*
  - *That's their problem.*
  - *It was a bad company.*
  - *My boss was a real jerk.*
  - *The college wasn't very good.*
  - *They told me to do it that way.*
  - *I can't remember why I did that.*
  - *No one there appreciated my work.*
  - *I didn't have time to visit your website.*
  - *I'm not a job hopper – I'm getting lots of experience.*

The last two excuses can be very revealing. Surprisingly, many interviewees fail to do their homework and visit the website of a perspective employer. There's simply no excuse for failing to do this other than laziness or disinterest. If you didn't have time to visit the website, then perhaps the employer doesn't have time to take you seriously. If you are a serial job hopper – averaging more than one job every one to two years – you better put together a very convincing story to dispel any suspicions that you are likely to leave this employer shortly, too. Lame excuses won't work. Why invest time and money in someone who plans to soon leave? Why would an employer want to train you for your next job with another employer? Do you know what it costs to replace an employee? One to two times your base salary! Job hoppers simply are not welcomed by many employers, other than ones who anticipate a high employee turnover in their industry, such as retail stores, restaurants, construction, and other low-wage blue-collar and service industry positions.

4. **Presents a poor appearance and negative image.** Dresses inappropriately for the interview – under-dresses or over-dresses for the position or the time of day. Offers a limp and sweaty handshake, emits irritating odors (from perfumes to bad breath and body odor), over-decorates with jewelry and body art (tattoos), looks extremely overweight, or appears too old or too young for the job. He or she may need to learn some basic grooming habits, from haircut and style to makeup and nails, or undergo a major makeover.

5. **Expresses bad, negative, and corrosive attitudes.** Tends to be negative, overbearing, extremely aggressive, cynical, and opinionated to the extreme. Expresses intolerance and strong prejudices toward others. Complains a lot about everything and everybody. Indicates a possible caustic personality that will not fit in well with the company. Regardless of how talented this person may be, unless he works in a cell by himself, he'll probably be fired within two months for having a bad attitude that pollutes the office and harms morale. **Attitude is everything** in a job interview. It reveals your motivation and enthusiasm to do the job as well as indicates how you probably make decisions and deal with others.

6. **Engages in inappropriate and unexpected behaviors for an interview situation.** Shows off scars, tattoos, muscles, or pictures of family. Slouches in the chair. Tells inappropriate jokes. Expresses extreme opinions. Picks up items on the interviewer's desk. Flirts with the interviewer. Possibly an exhibitionist who may also want to date the boss and harass co-workers!

7. **Appears somewhat incoherent and unfocused.** Tends to offer incomplete thoughts, loses focus, and jumps around to unrelated ideas. Hard to keep a focused conversation going. Incoherent thought processes indicate a possible attention deficit disorder (ADD) problem or some other disability, such as a drug or alcohol addiction, that could be detrimental to performing the job.

8. **Inarticulate.** Speaks poorly, from sound of voice and diction to grammar, vocalized pauses, and jargon. Uses lots of *"you know," "ah," "like," "okay,"* and *"well"* fillers. Expresses a low-class or age-inappropriate street language – *"cool," "damn," "man," "wow."* Not a good candidate for using the telephone or interacting with clients. Appears verbally illiterate or wired for failure.

9. **Gives short, incomplete, and/or vague and uncertain answers to questions.** Tends to respond to most questions with *"Yes," "No," "Maybe," "I'm not sure,"* or *"That's an interesting idea"* when the interviewer expects more in-depth and decisive answers. Appears shallow and indicates a lack of substance, initiative, interest, and enthusiasm. Indicates a high degree of uncertainly in making decisions – not a good action-oriented candidate who needs to make quick and smart decisions based on limited information.

10. **Lacks a sense of direction.** When asked where he sees himself five years from now, has difficulty giving a thoughtful answer. Appears to have no goals or apparent objectives beyond "a job." Apparently he is just looking for another job and paycheck rather than pursuing a passion or cause. Little indication the

candidate is self-motivated. This one will probably watch the clock all day long and require lots of close supervision and direction, which creates another unnecessary job!

11. **Appears ill or has a possible undisclosed medical condition.** Looks pale, glassy-eyed, gaunt, or yellow. Coughs, sneezes, and sounds terrible. Volunteers information about some past health issues and talks about his upcoming operation – within six weeks of starting the job! Suspects this person may have an illness or a drug and alcohol addiction that could be costly to the company and detrimental to doing the job.

12. **Volunteers personal information that normally would be illegal or inappropriate to ask.** Candidate makes interviewer feel uncomfortable by talking about religion, politics, age, family, divorce, sexual orientation, or physical and mental health. Volunteers the fact that she hopes to soon start a family, she currently receives unemployment benefits, spouse is in jail, she is in the process of getting a divorce, or she is a single or unwed mother with two small children. In response to "tell me about yourself," the interviewee focuses almost solely on **personal** rather than professional matters – birthplace, schools, family, hobbies, sports interests, and travel plans. The interviewer finds all these facts "interesting" but of little relevance to the job in question. Some of the personal and lifestyle information raises red flags.

13. **Emits bad or irritating smells.** Reeks of excessive perfume, cologne, or shaving lotion – could kill mosquitos! Can smell smoke or alcohol on breath. Strong body odor indicates personal hygiene issues. Has bad breath throughout the interview, which gets cut short by the employer for an "unexplained" reason. Interviewer concludes this candidate just doesn't smell right for the job! He's sure fellow workers and clients would agree with his assessment.

14. **Shows little enthusiasm, drive, or initiative.** Appears to be just looking for a job, putting in time, and collecting a paycheck. Tends to be passive and indifferent most of the time and a self-

centered wise guy some of the time. No evidence of being a self-starter who takes initiative and solves problems on his own. Not sure what motivates this person other than close supervision and possible threats of termination. Indeed, he'll require constant supervision and direction. The company will have an employee with lots of play-time on his hands or this will soon become a case where the job expands to fill the time allotted. He'll become the "job guy" who always says *"I did my job just like you told me,"* but not much beyond what's assigned. Don't expect much from this person, who will probably be overpaid for what he produces and who may create more problems that will need to be solved by other employees.

15. **Lacks confidence and self-esteem.** Seems unsure of self, nervous, and ill at ease. When asked *"What if…"* and *"Give me an example of a time when you…"* questions, has difficulty coming up with good responses that indicate an ability to produce outcomes and provide leadership. Intellectually curious but not good at closure. Appears somewhat academic: thinks a lot about issues but has difficulty in quickly drawing conclusions and taking action. Lacks decisiveness in making decisions – a real time killer when it comes time to participate in meetings and work in teams. Communicates uncertainty with such comments as *"I don't know," "Maybe," "I'm not sure," "Hadn't really thought of that," "Interesting question," "I'll have to think about that,"* or redirects with the question *"Well, what do you think?"* Not good leadership and team building material.

16. **Appears too eager and hungry for the job.** Is overly enthusiastic, engages in extreme flattery, gives self-centered answers to many interview questions, and appears suspiciously nervous. Early in the interview, before learning much about the company or job, makes such comments as *"I really like it here," "I really need this job," "Is there overtime?," "What are you paying?," "How many vacation days do you give?"* Something does not feel right about this candidate. The gut feeling is that this one is likely to be more trouble than he is worth!

17. **Communicates dishonesty or deception.** Uses canned interview language, evades probing questions, frequently changes the subject, and appears disingenuous. Looks like a tricky character who has things to hide and thus will probably be sneaky and deceptive on the job. When asked why he worked for three different employers during the past four years, says he had the misfortunate of being "laid off." Quickly changes the subject rather than give details on why he was chosen for the layoffs. Something is not right here.

18. **Demonstrates extreme role-playing to the point of being too smooth and superficial.** Dresses nicely, has a firm handshake and good eye contact, answers most questions okay, appears enthusiastic, and keeps repeating the same redundant 30-second storyline about his key strengths – just like some irritating interview books and videos tell job seekers to do. But when asked more substantive *"What if"* and behavior-based questions, or requested to give examples of specific accomplishments, the candidate seems to be caught off balance and stumbles, giving incomplete answers or repeating that same 30-second storyline that question his ability to think on his feet or move outside the mental box he has put himself in. Can't put one's finger on the problem, but the gut reaction is that this role-playing candidate is very superficial and will probably end up being the "dressed for success" and "coached for the interview" employee from hell!

19. **Appears evasive when asked about possible problems with background.** Gives evasive answers or tries to change the subject in reference to red flag questions about lack of skills and experience, limited education, frequent job changes, termination, and time gaps in work history. Such responses raise questions about the interviewee's honesty, credibility, responsibility, and overall behavior. Indicates a possible negative behavior pattern that probably needs further investigation.

20. **Speaks negatively of previous employers and co-workers.** When asked why she left previous employers, usually responds by bad-mouthing them. Has little good to say about others who

apparently were not as important as this candidate. Does not appear to be a team player. Seems to be very self-centered and arrogant.

21. **Maintains poor eye contact.** Candidate has "shifty eyes" that raise suspicions about his truthfulness and forthrightness. While he may be shy, his vague answers to questions accompanied by irritating eye contact sends mixed verbal/nonverbal messages that disrupt the flow of the interview.

    At least in America, eye contact is viewed as an indication of trustworthiness and attention. Individuals who fail to maintain an appropriate amount of eye contact are often judged as untrustworthy – have something to hide. Having too little or too much eye contact during the interview gives off mixed messages about what the candidate is saying. Worst of all, it may make the interviewer feel uncomfortable in the interviewee's presence.

22. **Offers a limp or overly firm handshake.** Interviewers often get two kinds of handshakes from candidates – the wimps and the bone-crushers. Your initial handshake may be viewed as saying something about your personality. Candidates offering a cold, wet, and limp handshake often come across as corpses! Bone-crushers may appear too aggressive.

23. **Comes unprepared and shows little interest in the company.** Indicates he didn't do much research, since he knows little about the company and didn't take time to check out the company's website. Asks this killer question: *"What do you do here?"* Few answers to questions relate to the interests of the company. Fails to ask questions that would indicate an interest in the job or the company.

24. **Talks about salary and benefits early in the interview.** Rather than try to learn more about the company and position as well as demonstrate her value (she does say she can easily do the job), the candidate seems preoccupied with salary and benefits by talking about them within the first 15 minutes of the interview. Shows little interest in the job or employer beyond the compensation package.

Interviewers read between the lines for red flags. When an interviewee prematurely talks about compensation, a big red flag goes up. Such a line of questioning usually indicates this is a self-centered candidate who is not really interested in doing the job. Their primary interest is salary and benefits.

25. **Is discourteous, ill-mannered, and disrespectful.** Arrives for the interview a half hour late with no explanation or a phone call indicating a problem en route. Just sits and waits for the interviewer to ask questions. Picks up things on the interviewer's desk. Challenges the interviewer's ideas. Closes the interview without thanking the interviewer for the opportunity to interview for the job. Not even going to charm and etiquette school would help this candidate!

26. **Appears socially awkward.** Seems to have difficulty meeting people, maintaining good eye contact, and sustaining even a short conversation. The clothes, shoes, and jewelry don't seem to fit right or come together well. Appears uncomfortable in the presence of others. Table manners and drinking behavior leave much to be desired.

27. **Tells inappropriate jokes and laughs a lot.** Attempts at humor bomb – appears to be a smart ass who likes to laugh at his own jokes. Comes across as an irritating clown who says stupid and silly things. Will need to isolate this one to keep him away from other employees who don't share such humor and tastelessness.

28. **Talks too much.** Can't answer a question without droning on and on with lots of irrelevant talk. Volunteers all kinds of information, including interesting but sensitive personal observations and gossip the interviewer neither needs nor wants. Doesn't know when to shut up. Would probably waste a lot of valuable work time talking, talking, and talking and thus irritating other employees. Seems to need lots of social strokes through talk, which she readily initiates.

29. Argues with the interviewer. Disagrees with interviewer about management philosophy, marketing approaches, new initiatives, and the job search. Appears to have a contentious personality that is likely to clash with other members of the team he'll be working with.

30. Drops names to impress the interviewer. Talks about all the important people he knows who are his "friends." Tells stories about how important he is to those people and how much they admire him. Unclear how such name-dropping relates to the job in question. Perhaps he thinks the interviewer will be impressed with a verbal Rolodex of who he knows.

But interviewers tend to be put off by such candidates who, instead, appear to be insecure, arrogant, and patronizing – three deadly sins that may shorten your interview from 45 minutes to 15 minutes! The truth about the extent of their "friendship" with such people is suspect. If they know the candidate well, why are they not included on the candidate's list of references?

31. Appears needy and greedy. Talks a lot about financial needs and compensation. When discussing salary, talks about his personal financial situation, including debts and planned future purchases, rather than what the job is worth and what value he will bring to the job. Seems to expect the employer is interested in supporting his lifestyle, which may be a combination of irresponsible financial behavior, failing to plan, living beyond his pay grade, and having bad luck. This line of talk indicates he probably has debilitating financial problems that go far beyond the salary level of this job. A background check may indicate financial difficulties.

32. Closes the interview by just leaving. When asked if she has any questions, says *"No"* and gets up and leaves after shaking hands and saying *"Thank you for meeting with me."*

Most interviewees fail to properly close interviews. How you close the interview may determine whether or not you will be invited back to another interview or offered the job. Never ever end the interview with this stupid and presumptuous closing prior to being offered the job: *"So when can I start?"* This question will likely finish off the interview and your candidacy – you're back to being needy and greedy! Also, don't play the pressure game, even if it's true, by stating *"I have another interview this week. When can I expect to hear from you?"* One other critical element to this close: send a nice thank-you letter within 24 hours in which you again express your appreciation for the interview and your interest in the job.

33. Fails to talk about accomplishments. Candidate concentrates on explaining work history as primarily consisting of assigned duties and responsibilities. When asked to give examples of her three major accomplishments in her last jobs, doesn't seem to understand the question, gives little evidence of performance, or reverts once again to discussing formal duties and responsibilities. When probed further for accomplishments, doesn't really say much and shows discomfort about this line of questioning.

34. Does not ask questions about the job or employer. Seems to view the interview as a forum to which he has come to answer the interviewer's questions. When asked *"Do you have any questions?,"* the candidate replies *"No"* or *"You've covered everything."*

Asking questions is often more important to getting the job than answering questions. Your questions should focus on learning more about the position, job, and employer. When you ask thoughtful questions, you emphasize your interest in the employer and job as well as indicate your intelligence – qualities employers look for in candidates. Most important of all, you acquire critical information from which to decide whether or not you really want the job!

35. Too effusive and self-effacing. Appears nervous and overly anxious to please the interviewer by being extremely deferential and self-effacing. Has difficulty giving simple and straightforward answers to questions. Seems to lack self-confidence and thus appears compelled to go into unnecessary detail while answering questions. Doesn't know when it is appropriate to stop talking and move on to other more important matters. Such behaviors raise suspicions about the candidate – what's really beneath the surface?

36. Appears self-centered rather than employer-centered. Candidate appears to be preoccupied with himself, focusing on benefits he will receive rather than contributions he is likely to make to the organization. This orientation becomes immediately apparent by the direction of the answers and questions coming from the interviewee. It reveals a great deal about his motivations and possible work behavior. If the candidate primarily focuses on employee benefits, he will be perceived as self-centered. For example, a candidate who frequently uses "I" when talking about himself and the job may be very self-centered. On the other hand, the candidate who talks about "we" and "you" is usually more employer-oriented. Contrast these paired statements about the job and compensation:

> *"What would I be doing in this position?"*

> *"What do you see us achieving over the next six months?"*

> or

> *"What would I be making on this job?"*

> *"What do you normally pay for someone with my qualifications?"*

37. Demonstrates poor listening skills. Doesn't listen carefully to questions or seems to have her own agenda that overrides the interviewer's interest. Tends to go off in different directions from the questions being asked. Not a very empathetic listener both verbally and nonverbally. Seems to be more interested in talking about own agenda than focusing on the issues at hand. Apparently wants to take charge of the interview and be the Lone Ranger. The job really does require good listening skills!

38. **Seems not bright enough for the job.** Answering simple interview questions is like taking an intelligence test. Candidate has difficulty talking about past accomplishments. Doesn't seem to grasp what the job is all about or the skills required. Seems confused and lacks focus. Should never have gotten to the job interview but had a terrific looking resume that was probably written by a professional resume writer!

39. **Fails to know his/her worth and negotiate properly when it comes time to talk about compensation.** Candidate talks about salary and benefits early the interview. When salary is discussed, he appears to be fine with the first figure offered.

   Job seekers are well advised to only talk about salary and benefits **after** being offered the job. If you prematurely talk about compensation, you may diminish your value as well as appear self-centered. Be sure to research salary comparables so you know what you are worth in today's job market (start with www.salary.com). Listen carefully throughout the interview and ask questions that would give you a better idea of what the job is actually worth. Stress throughout the interview your skills and accomplishments – those things that are most valued by employers who are willing to pay what's necessary for top talent. When you do start negotiating, let the **employer** state a salary figure first and then negotiate using salary ranges to reach common ground.

40. **Fails to properly prepare for the interview.** This is the most important mistake of all. It affects all the other mistakes. Indeed, failing to prepare will immediately show when the candidate makes a bad first impression, fails to indicate knowledge about the company and job, fails to give good answers to standard interview questions, does not ask thoughtful questions, prematurely talks about salary and benefits, and leaves the interview without closing properly. In other words, the candidate makes many of the mistakes outlined above because he or she failed to anticipate what goes into a winning interview.

Tips From the Experts

Numerous print and online resources can help you avoid many of the mistakes outlined in this chapter. If you need help in preparing for the job interview, we recommend the following resources, which offer a wealth of tips on improving your job interview skills:

Books

101 Dynamite Questions to Ask at Your Job Interview
101 Great Answers to the Toughest Interview Questions
250 Job Interview Questions You'll Most Likely Be Asked
301 Smart Answers to Tough Interview Questions
Adams Job Interview Almanac, with CD-ROM
Boost Your Interview I.Q.
Don't Blow the Interview
Haldane's Best Answers to Tough Interview Questions
How to Ace the Brain Teaser Interview
Interview Magic
Interview Power
Interview Rehearsal Book
Job Interview Tips for People With Not-So-Hot Backgrounds
Job Interviews for Dummies
KeyWords to Nail Your Job Interview
Monster Careers: Interviewing
Nail the Job Interview!
Naked at the Interview
Perfect Phrases for the Perfect Interview
Power Interviews
Savvy Interviewing
Winning the Interview Game
Winning Job Interview
You've Got the Interview

Websites

- Monster.com   http://interview.monster.com
- About.com   http://about.com/jobsearch/interview
                       resources

- InterviewPro   www.interviewpro.com
- Job-Interview.net   www.job-interview.net
- Interview Coach   www.interviewcoach.com
- Quintessential Careers   www.quintcareers.com/intvres.html
- Wetfeet.com   www.wetfeet.com/Article%20Types/
                              Interviewing.aspx
- Collegegrad.com   www.collegegrad.com/video/college
                              grad.shtml

3

What's Your Interview IQ?

W HILE EFFECTIVE RESUMES, letters, and networking are keys to getting job interviews, you must perform well in the interview in order to get the job offer. Just how well prepared are you for the job interview? Do you have the right attitudes, skills, and abilities to get job interviews as well as perform well throughout what may well become multiple job interviews for a single position?

Let's quickly assess your interview skills and abilities by indicating your degree of agreement/disagreement to the following statements:

SCALE:	5 = Strongly agree	2 = Disagree
	4 = Agree	1 = Strongly disagree
	3 = Maybe, not certain	

1. I know what skills I can offer employers.　　　5　4　3　2　1

2. I know what skills employers most seek
   in candidates.　　　5　4　3　2　1

3. I can clearly explain to employers what
   I do well and enjoy doing.　　　5　4　3　2　1

4. I can explain in 60 seconds why an
   employer should hire me.   5   4   3   2   1

5. I can identify and target employers
   I want to get an interview with.   5   4   3   2   1

6. I can develop a job referral network.   5   4   3   2   1

7. I can prospect for job leads.   5   4   3   2   1

8. I can generate at least one job interview
   for every 10 job search contacts I make.   5   4   3   2   1

9. I can follow up on job interviews.   5   4   3   2   1

10. After receiving a job offer, I can persuade
    an employer to re-examine my salary
    after six months on the job.   5   4   3   2   1

11. I know which questions interviewers are
    most likely to ask me.   5   4   3   2   1

12. If asked to reveal my weaknesses, I know
    how to respond – answer honestly, but
    always stress my strengths.   5   4   3   2   1

13. I know how to best dress for the interview. 5 4   3   2   1

14. I know the various types of interviews I may
    encounter and how to appropriately respond
    in each situation.   5   4   3   2   1

15. I can easily approach strangers for job
    information and advice.   5   4   3   2   1

16. I know where to find information on
    organizations that are most likely to be
    interested in my skills.   5   4   3   2   1

17. I know how to go beyond vacancy announce-
    ments to locate job opportunities appropriate
    for my qualifications.   5   4   3   2   1

18. I know how to interview appropriate
    people for job information and advice.   5   4   3   2   1

19. I know many people who can refer me to
    others for informational interviews.   5   4   3   2   1

20. I can uncover jobs on the hidden job market.   5   4   3   2   1

21. I know how to prepare and practice for the
    critical job interview.   5   4   3   2   1

22. I know how to stress my positives.   5   4   3   2   1

23. I know how to research the organization and
    individuals who are likely to interview me.   5   4   3   2   1

24. I have considered how I would respond to
    illegal questions posed by prospective
    employers.   5   4   3   2   1

25. I can telephone effectively for job leads.   5   4   3   2   1

26. I am prepared to conduct an effective
    telephone interview.   5   4   3   2   1

27. I know when and how to deal with salary
    questions.   5   4   3   2   1

28. I know what to read while waiting in the
    outer office prior to the interview.   5   4   3   2   1

29. I can nonverbally communicate my interest
    and enthusiasm for the job.   5   4   3   2   1

30. I know the best time to arrive at the
    interview site.   5   4   3   2   1

31. I know how to respond using positive form
    and content as well as supports when
    responding to interviewers' questions.   5   4   3   2   1

32. I know how to summarize my strengths
    and value at the close of the interview.   5   4   3   2   1

33. I know what to include in a thank-you letter.   5   4   3   2   1

34. I know when and how to follow up the
    job interview.   5   4   3   2   1

35. I know what do during the 24- to 48-hour
    period following a job offer.   5   4   3   2   1

36. I can clearly explain to interviewers what
    I like and dislike about particular jobs.   5   4   3   2   1

37. I can explain to interviewers why I made
    my particular educational choices, including
    my major and grade point average.   5   4   3   2   1

38. I can clearly explain to interviewers what
    I want to be doing 5 or 10 years from now.   5   4   3   2   1

39. I have a list of references who can speak in
    a positive manner about me and my work
    abilities.   5   4   3   2   1

40. I can clearly state my job and career
    objectives as both skills and outcomes.   5   4   3   2   1

41. I have set aside 20 hours a week to primarily
    conduct informational interviews.   5   4   3   2   1

42. I know what foods and drinks are best to
    select if the interview includes a luncheon
    or dinner meeting.   5   4   3   2   1

43. I know how to listen effectively.   5   4   3   2   1

44. I can explain why an employer should hire me. 5   4   3   2   1

45. I am prepared to handle the salary question
    at whatever point it comes up.   5   4   3   2   1

46. I know when to use my resume in an
    informational interview.   5   4   3   2   1

47. I can generate three new job leads each day.   5   4   3   2   1

48. I can outline my major achievements in my
     last three jobs and show how they relate to
     the job I am interviewing for.   5   4   3   2   1

49. I know what the interviewer is looking for
     when he or she asks about my weaknesses.   5   4   3   2   1

50. I am prepared to handle panel, serial, stress,
     behavioral, and situational interviews.   5   4   3   2   1

TOTAL I.Q.

Once you have completed this exercise, add your responses to compute a total score. This will comprise your composite I.Q. If your score is between 200 and 250, you seem well prepared to successfully handle the interview. If your score is between 150 and 199, you are heading in the right direction, and many of our recommended resources should help you increase your interview competencies. If your score falls below 150, you have a great deal of work to do in preparation for the job interview. Subsequent chapters should help you substantially increase your interview IQ.

4

I Hate Interviews!
Attitude and Preparation
Count the Most

WE HAVE YET TO MEET anyone who really loves to interview. After all, a job interview is like a blind date that could quickly turn into a nervous honeymoon followed by a problematic marriage and ugly divorce. An interview is all about developing a new relationship that hopefully becomes mutually beneficial. Central to developing that relationship is your attitude.

For employers and interviewers, the whole hiring process is expensive, time consuming, and fraught with anxiety, uncertainty, and risks. Most employers have better things to do with their time than to go on several blind dates in the hopes of finding the right mate. Indeed, most dislike having to evaluate resumes, applications and letters, meet candidates, ask and answer questions, and go through the whole process of deciding whether candidate A, B, C, D, or E best meets their needs. After hours and weeks of assessing candidates to determine who is the best fit for the job, employers are still not sure if they made the right decision. Only time will tell the truth as the individual settles into the position and company.

Persuading Strangers to Take Action

For job seekers, interviews are high-anxiety activities. Stress, trust, and the fear of failure characterize the many mixed emotions of interviewees.

27

For them, the interview is all about persuading strangers to take actions they ordinarily would not – offer you a job. Employers must **trust** that you will bring **value** to their organization in exchange for position, money, and benefits. At the same time, you must **trust** that the organization will be a **good fit** for your interests, skills, and motivations.

While most job seekers are eager to get a job interview, few of them look forward to actually going to job interviews. Indeed, the joy of getting that phone call asking you to meet for an interview is quickly tempered with the fear of not doing well in the job interview. Getting the interview means you will soon, maybe within 24 hours, be meeting strangers who will closely assess your potential to do the job. They will ask you numerous questions about your background, experiences, likes and dislikes, decision-making abilities, and goals. You also may encounter personality tests and trick questions that could quickly derail your candidacy. You'll also be competing with other candidates who ostensibly may be better qualified for the job. You may

> *A job interview is like a blind date that could quickly turn into a nervous honeymoon followed by a problematic marriage and possible divorce.*

be interviewed by several key individuals as well as invited back for five or six additional interviews before being offered the job. And the job offer, if you get it, may be less than what you expect.

No wonder most job seekers approach the job interview with trepidation – a combination of sweaty palms, dry throat, and fear of rejection. Just getting to the interview stage has taken a lot of work. You've been trying to persuade employers to meet with you. Now that you got the interview, how do you plan to prepare for it? Do you know how to get to the interview site on time? What will you wear and take with you? How will you greet the interviewer and engage in small talk? How will you communicate that you are the best candidate for the job? What will you say and do during the interview that will convince them that **you** should be offered the job rather than someone else?

Attitude and Preparation Are Everything

If you approach the interview with negative expectations, chances are you will hate going to a job interview and appear less than enthusiastic about the job. Your fear of rejection may set you up for failure as you neglect to properly prepare for the job interview.

We recommend that you approach the job interview with a **positive attitude** and **extensive preparation** – this is an important challenge from which you can and will excel. The following tips serve as prerequisites for preparing for the job interview. They emphasize the importance of attitude and orientation in overcoming rejections.

TIP #1
Expect and welcome numerous rejections along the road to success.

QUESTIONS: Are you sometimes reluctant to contact people for fear of being rejected? Do you expect to be turned down for a job interview or passed over for the job? Do you take rejections personally, as an indication of failure? Do you avoid situations that may result in a great deal of competition or possible failure? Do you look for the easy way out of challenging situations?

IF YES: The fear of rejections remains a major deterrent for maintaining a positive and proactive job search. As most successful people will admit, failure is part of the success game. Indeed, while the road to success is often paved with failures, your destination is best navigated through drive and persistence. As any successful salesperson will tell you, failures in the form of rejections are all part of the selling game. And engaging in a

> *While the road to success is often paved with rejections, your destination is best navigated through drive and persistence.*

job interview is the ultimate exercise in personal salesmanship – you are trying to sell a product (you) to a potential buyer (an employer). Few job seekers can handle numerous rejections. They take them as signs of personal failure and thus become discouraged, even depressed, after receiving just three or four rejections. They have difficulty maintaining a positive attitude as well as exuding energy and enthusiasm in the face of multiple rejections. After a few rejections, they lose the will to go on and thus begin cutting corners and rationalizing their failure to persist in routinizing the most important steps in their job search. Some repeat the lament of the frustrated job seeker – *"No one will hire me!"*

Let's face it. Few people can maintain the same high level of energy, enthusiasm, and motivation throughout a three- to six-month job search. It's especially difficult when they encounter numerous rejections along the way. Indeed, the number one problem most job seekers encounter and have difficulty dealing with is rejections. Accustomed to being successful in other aspects of their lives, they find a job search can be very ego-deflating and depressing. In fact, most people can handle three rejections in a row, but four, five, six, or seven rejections are difficult to deal with. Faced with a string of rejections, many job seekers become demoralized, cut back on their job search activities, or just go through the motions of looking for a job by sending out more resumes and letters in response to classified ads and online job postings.

TIPS: There are certain things you can do to keep yourself focused and motivated. First, **treat rejections as part of the job search game**. You should welcome them as a necessary element in the whole process of achieving success. You can't get acceptances before acquiring numerous rejections. Consider the typical job search which goes something like this:

No, No, No, No, No, No, Maybe, No, No, No, Yes, No, No, No
No, No, No, Maybe, No, Maybe, Yes, No, No, No, No, Yes, Yes

If you get disillusioned and quit after receiving four rejections, you will prematurely fail. You need to continue "collecting" more rejections in order to get an acceptance. In fact, we often recommend that individuals get up in the morning with the idea of collecting at least 20 rejections! You will eventually get acceptances, but you must first deal with many rejections on the road to success. How you handle rejections may largely determine how successful you will be in your job search, career, and life. If you identify what it is you want to do but cannot implement the necessary changes because you fear rejection, you will be going nowhere with your future.

Second, **reward yourself after achieving certain goals**. For example, let's say your goal this week is to send out 20 resumes, make 35 networking calls, and arrange four informational interviews. If you start on Monday and achieve these goals by Thursday, reward yourself by taking Friday off or going out for dinner at your favorite restaurant. Try to build a system of rewards related to specific goals so that you can occasionally celebrate successes. These little rewards will help keep you focused and motivated throughout your job search. Remember, this is a **process** that takes time and requires a positive approach to handling rejections. Give each job search encounter your best effort but be sure to move on to other potential opportunities.

TIP #2
Approach the job interview as an opportunity to both showcase your positives and learn about the job and employer.

QUESTIONS: Do you view the job interview as a form of gamesmanship involving winners and losers? Is your primary purpose to get a job offer? Do you feel a lot of competitive pressure when interviewing for a job? Are you preoccupied with giving the "right answers" to interview questions? Do you question your performance during the interview?

IF YES: You may be setting yourself up for interview anxiety and potential failure. Indeed, you may show your nervousness because you are primarily focused on **yourself** – preoccupied with trying to impress the interviewer with answers to questions. This is one place you **must** get over yourself and primarily focus on the interviewer and the job.

The number one reason interviewees get nervous and stumble during interviews is the fact that they primarily focus on themselves rather than on the interviewer. Ironically, their internal voice conducts a secondary interview with themselves by constantly asking these interfering and self-defeating evaluation questions:

- *How am I doing?*
- *Did I answer that question right?*
- *Should I have said something else?*
- *Am I making a good impression?*
- *Do they like me?*

When you approach the interview in this manner, you neglect three of the most important skills employers look for in employees – the ability to listen, learn, and respond extemporaneously.

TIPS: You should be focused on the interviewer and the job rather than on yourself and how well you are performing in the interview in order to get the job offer. Rather than trying to dish out canned answers, keyword phrases, or clever scripts to anticipated interview questions, you should demonstrate strong listening, learning, and **extemporaneous speaking** skills. When you do this, you will lessen your anxiety and nervousness and present an image of someone who is interested, creative, thoughtful, and engaging. You have something new and important to say that reflects on your ability to do the job better than anyone else. You become **memorable** because your verbal and nonverbal behaviors set you apart from the less impressive competition. In the job interview, **being remembered in a positive manner** is the next best thing to being offered a job!

A job interview should be a **learning experience** for both parties involved rather than a game of winners and losers. The employer needs to know if you are the right "fit" for the position. The fact that you were invited to a job interview means that you probably already have the necessary qualifications for the job. Now it's time to determine if you meet other qualifying, yet unstated, criteria – do you have the right attitude, personality, trustworthiness, creativity, and decision-making ability to fit into the company culture? Do you have the enthusiasm, energy, and passion to do great things in this company? Are you likable? Are you better than the other candidates?

At the same time, you need to know if you want to invest your time and effort with this organization. Is it the type of place you want to be associated with during the next three to five years? Will it provide opportunities for you to make significant contributions and grow as both an individual and professional? Will it use your major strengths or require you to showcase your weaknesses? Will it be an exciting place to work?

TIP #3
Focus on developing a positive attitude toward both the job interview and the employer.

QUESTIONS: Do you tend to say negative things about others, especially your bosses and co-workers? Do you hang around depressing people who use lots of negative terms such as *"can't," "won't,"* and *"shouldn't"*? Do you often talk yourself out of doing things because you believe something negative will happen as a consequence? Do you express negative thoughts to others who may find that you are a depressing person to hang around? Do you avoid doing certain things because you are afraid of rejections? Are you sometimes envious of people who seem to have a positive outlook on life and who appear to be very successful?

IF YES: This is not the time to be cocky, assertive, arrogant, or self-centered. People with negative attitudes tend to attract negative outcomes. Take, for example, the job search, which is all about making good first impressions on strangers who know little or nothing about your background, capabilities, and personality. Whether completing an application, writing a resume, or interviewing for a job, you will reveal your attitude in many different ways, both verbally and nonverbally.

Many job seekers show attitudes of disrespect, deceit, laziness, irresponsibility, and carelessness – all red flags that will quickly knock you out of the competition. Such attitudes are communicated during the critical job interview when employers read both verbal and nonverbal behavioral cues. Here are some common mistakes job seekers make that show off some killer attitudes that also reflect on their character:

Mistake	Attitude/Character
▪ Lacks a job objective	Confused and unfocused
▪ Misspells words on resume, application, and/or letter	Careless and inconsiderate
▪ Uses poor grammar	Uneducated
▪ Sends resume to wrong person	Careless and error-prone
▪ Arrives late for job interview	Unreliable
▪ Dresses inappropriately	Unperceptive and insensitive
▪ Knows little about company	Lazy, thoughtless, or uninterested
▪ Talks about salary and benefits	Greedy and self-centered
▪ Badmouths former employer	Disrespectful and angry
▪ Doesn't admit to weaknesses	Disingenuous and calculating
▪ Boasts about himself	Obnoxious and self-centered
▪ Lies about background	Deceitful and dishonest
▪ Lacks eye contact	Untrustworthy and shifty
▪ Blames others for problems	Irresponsible
▪ Interrupts and argues	Inconsiderate and inflexible
▪ Has trouble answering questions	Unprepared and nervous
▪ Fails to ask any questions	Uninterested in job
▪ Jumps from one extreme to another	Manic and disorganized
▪ Fails to close and follow up interview	Doesn't care about the job

On the other hand, employers look for attitudes that indicate a candidate has some of the following positive characteristics:

- Accurate
- Adaptable
- Careful
- Competent
- Considerate
- Cooperative
- Dependable
- Determined
- Diligent
- Discreet
- Educated
- Efficient
- Empathic
- Energetic
- Enthusiastic
- Fair
- Focused
- Good-natured
- Happy
- Helpful
- Honest
- Intelligent
- Loyal

- Nice
- Open-minded
- Patient
- Perceptive
- Precise
- Predictable
- Prompt
- Purposeful
- Reliable
- Resourceful
- Respectful
- Responsible
- Self-motivated
- Sensitive
- Sincere
- Skilled
- Tactful
- Team player
- Tenacious
- Tolerant
- Trustworthy
- Warm

TIPS: If you have negative attitudes, you are probably an unhappy person. It's time you took control of both your attitudes and behaviors. Start by identifying several of your negative attitudes and try to transform them into positive attitudes. As you do this, you will begin to identify the positive person you want to be. For starters, examine these sets of negative and positive attitudes that can arise at various stages of the job search, especially during the critical job interview:

Negative Attitude	**Positive Attitude**
I didn't like my last employer.	*It was time for me to move on to a more progressive company.*
I haven't been able to find a job in over three months. I really want this one.	*I've been learning a great deal during the past several weeks of my job search.*

My last two jobs were problems.	*I learned a great deal about what I really love to do from those last two jobs.*
Do you have a job for me?	*I'm in the process of conducting a job search. Do you know anyone who might have an interest in someone with my qualifications?*
I can't come in for an interview tomorrow since I'm interviewing for another job. What about Wednesday? That looks good.	*I have a conflict tomorrow. Wednesday would be good. Could we do something in the morning?*
Yes, I flunked out of college in my sophomore year.	*After two years in college I decided to pursue a career in computer sales.*
I really hated studying math.	*Does this job require math?*
Sorry about that spelling error on my resume. I was never good at spelling.	(Doesn't point it out; if asked, said *"It's one that got away."*)
I don't enjoy working in teams.	*I work best when given an assignment that allows me to work alone.*
What does this job pay?	*How does the pay scale here compare with other firms in the area?*
Will I have to work weekends?	*What are the normal hours for someone in this position?*
I have to see my parole officer once a month. Can I have that day off?	*I have an appointment I need to keep the last Friday of each month. Would it be okay if I took off three hours that day?*
I'm three months pregnant. Will your health care program cover my delivery?	*Could you tell me more about your benefits, such as health and dental care?*
I've just got out of prison and need a job.	*While incarcerated, I turned my life around by getting my GED, learning new skills, and controlling my anger.*

I'm really excited about becoming a landscape architect and working with your company.

Can you think of any particular negative attitudes you might have that you can restate in positive language? Identify five that relate to your job search and work. State them in both the negative and positive:

Negative Attitude   **Positive Attitude**

1. _____   _____

   _____   _____

   _____   _____

2. _____   _____

   _____   _____

   _____   _____

3. _____   _____

   _____   _____

   _____   _____

4. _____   _____

   _____   _____

   _____   _____

5. _____   _____

   _____   _____

   _____   _____

You'll find numerous books, audiotapes, videos, and software specializing in developing positive thinking. Most are designed to transform the thinking and perceptions of individuals by changing negative attitudes. One of the major themes underlying these products is that you can change your life through positive thinking. Individuals whose lives are troubled, for example, can literally transform themselves by changing their thinking in new and positive directions. These products are especially popular with people in sales careers who must constantly stay motivated and positive in the face of making cold calls that result in numerous rejections. Positive thinking helps them get through the day, the week, and the month despite numerous rejections that would normally dissuade most people from continuing to pursue more sales calls that result in even more rejections.

One of the most important books on self-transformation through positive thinking is Napoleon Hill's *Think and Grow Rich*. This single book has had a tremendous influence on the development of the positive thinking industry, which now includes hundreds of motivational speakers and gurus who produce numerous seminars, books, and audio programs for the true believers. Other popular authors and books include:

Keith Harrell	■ *Attitude Is Everything*
Napoleon Hill and W. Clement Stone	■ *Success Through a Positive Mental Attitude*
Dr. Norman Vincent Peale	■ *The Power of Positive Thinking* ■ *Six Attitudes for Winners*
Anthony Robbins	■ *Personal Power* ■ *Unlimited Power* ■ *Awaken the Giant Within* ■ *Live With Passion!*
Dr. Robert H. Schuller	■ *You Can Become the Person You Want to Be* ■ *Be Happy Attitudes*
Dale Carnegie	■ *How to Win Friends and Influence People*
Brian Tracy	■ *Change Your Thinking, Change Your Life* ■ *Create Your Own Future*

- *Eat That Frog!*
- *Focal Point*
- *Maximum Achievement*

David Schwartz   ▪ *The Magic of Thinking Big*

Zig Ziglar   ▪ *How to Get What You Want*

Og Mandino   ▪ *Secrets of Success*

Steve Chandler   ▪ *100 Ways to Motivate Yourself*
                            ▪ *Reinventing Yourself*

Bay and Macpherson   ▪ *Change Your Attitude*

As you will quickly discover, a positive attitude that focuses on the future is one of the most powerful motivators for achieving success. Any of these recommended books will get you started on the road to changing your attitudes as well as your life. They are filled with fascinating stories of self-transformation, motivational language, and exercises for developing positive attitudes for success.

Here's an important life-changing tip: Get serious about shaping your future by committing yourself to reading at least one of these books over the next two weeks. If reading is a problem for you, try to find audiotapes that include similar material. You can find the books and audiotapes in your local library. Set aside at least one hour each day to read a book or listen to a tape that can literally change your life. Such books and tapes will both exercise your mind and inspire you to be your best.

TIP #4
Always be polite and considerate to others.

QUESTIONS: Are you sometimes rude, disrespectful, and inconsiderate to others? Have you said things that cause you embarrassment? Do others try to avoid you or leave you out of conversations and meetings? Are you the last one to be chosen to participate in projects, team efforts, or social events? Do you talk about yourself a lot?

IF YES: Many people are oblivious to such negative behaviors and thus don't understand they are being silently ostracized by those they work with. Finding you irritating, they wish you would go away forever. Ask yourself these questions: Do you try to dominate conversations? Do you interrupt when someone else is talking? Do you enter an office without knocking or making an appointment? Do you use your cell phone for personal business while working with others? Do you talk loudly when others are trying to work? Do you make inappropriate jokes or comments to members of the opposite sex? Do you make negative comments to others about your boss? Do you tell your boss that you don't have time to do the assigned work or talk down to him or her? Do you dress differently from others in the company? Do you ask personal questions that are none of your business? Do you try to put other people down?

No one wants to work with someone who is rude, disrespectful, or inconsiderate. Rude employees are generally disliked by other employees who prefer not working with them. Rude and inconsiderate employees also alienate customers who will take their business elsewhere. If you have a pattern of rudeness and disrespect, you need a social and psychological makeover.

TIPS: People like individuals who are polite and considerate, observe social graces, ask good questions, and have important things to say. Carefully watch what you say and when and where you say it. Since it's impolite to interrupt other people, wait until others are finished before you begin talking. Better still, become a good listener – you'll learn more by listening than by talking! If you have something important to ask or tell someone, do so privately rather than distract others in the office with loud and disruptive conversation. Be polite by knocking on doors and asking permission before entering offices with closed doors. You might be a good candidate for a Dale Carnegie course related to his classic book *How to Win Friends and Influence People*. You need to acquire some important people skills so that others will like you rather than avoid you. In addition to the Dale Carnegie book, examine a few of their people-sensitive titles:

The Fine Art of Small Talk
How to Be a People Magnet
How to Make People Like You in 90 Seconds or Less
How to Start a Conversation and Make Friends
How to Talk to Anyone

Be sure to mind your social graces throughout the job interview – from the moment you arrive at the interview site until you exit the building. You want to leave the impression that you are someone others will enjoy working with.

TIP #5
Make your attitude the first thing you present
to the employer.

QUESTIONS: Do you have difficulty knowing what to do and say during a job interview? Do you lack energy and enthusiasm during a job interview? Do you have a negative or self-centered attitude that shows with strangers?

IF YES: Employers consistently report that attitude is one of the first things they notice in job candidates – attitude toward the job, toward themselves, toward previous employers, toward the interviewer, and toward life in general. Individuals with a negative or self-centered attitude are generally avoided by employers who prefer hiring individuals who have a positive and employer-centered attitude.

TIPS: Like the clothes you wear to an interview, your attitude is one of the first things employers see in candidates. Be sure you present a positive attitude in everything you do and say during the job interview. Keep focused on the employer and the job rather than on yourself and exude energy and enthusiasm throughout the job interview.

TIP #6
Take responsibility for your choices – no excuses.

QUESTIONS: Do you make excuses for questionable behaviors rather than accept responsibility? Is it always someone else who creates a problem or gets you into trouble? Do you usually come up with excuses for not doing things you should be doing?

IF YES: Sometimes it seems easier to place the blame for our shortcomings on others rather than to take responsibility for our own actions. If you were fired from a previous job, it was someone else's fault. Your boss "had it in for you" or you were the "fall guy" for someone else's mistake.

But most employers have heard the excuses before and are unimpressed and unconvinced. When a job candidate places the blame for his past problems on others, it says far more about the person making the excuse than about the person he is trying to blame.

We and other employers have often encountered 20 excuses related to the workplace. Some are even used by candidates during a job interview to explain their on-the-job behavior! Most of these excuses reflect an attitude lacking in responsibility and initiative:

1. No one told me.	11. I don't know how to do it.
2. I did what you said.	12. That's your problem.
3. Your directions were bad.	13. It wasn't very good.
4. It's not my fault.	14. Maybe you did it.
5. She did it.	15. I thought I wrote it down.
6. It just seemed to happen.	16. That's not my style.
7. It happens a lot.	17. He told me to do it that way.
8. What did he say?	18. I've got to go now.
9. I had a headache.	19. Where do you think it went?
10. I don't understand why.	20. We can talk about it later.

We all make excuses. Many are harmless excuses that help us get through a stressful day. Identify a few excuses you frequently make. What, for example, would you say to an interviewer if you arrived late for a job interview? What would you say if someone asks you why you dropped out of school, quit a job, or were fired from a job? Who was responsible for those actions?

When you offer excuses for your behavior, you literally show an attitude that is not appreciated by employers. Indeed, your attitude toward personal responsibility shows. People with positive attitudes and proactive behavior do not engage in behaviors that reflect such excuses. They have a "can do" attitude that focuses on the future. That attitude helps focus their minds on doing those things that are most important to achieving their goals. For example, rather than show up 10 minutes late for a job interview and say they got lost or had bad directions, people with positive attitudes and proactive behavior check out the interview location the day before in anticipation of arriving 10 minutes early. **They make no excuses because they plan ahead and engage in no-excuses behavior!**

TIPS: Take responsibility for mistakes you have made and learn from those experiences. In so doing, you will make a far better impression on the interviewer than you will by pointing your finger at someone else.

Enhance your credibility by indicating that you learned something from the situation that went wrong. You know the adage, *"When life gives you lemons, make lemonade."* You can turn a negative situation into a positive one and overcome a barrier by accepting responsibility, indicating what lessons you learned from it, and what you would do differently if faced with that or a similar situation in the future. You will make a far better impression than you will by shirking responsibility and placing the blame on someone else.

TIP #7
Focus with passion on your purpose in life.

QUESTIONS: Do you primarily try to give "correct" answers to interview questions – make up answers that you think interviewers want to hear? Do you appear uncertain as to what you want to do other than make more money and get more benefits? Do you lack goals and a purpose in life? Are you sometimes unhappy with your life? Do you wish you were a happier and more centered person? Are you uncertain what you want to do with the rest of your life? Do you lack focus and have trouble concentrating on your work? Do you often wander aimlessly from day to day, uncertain of your value and meaning in life? Do you sometimes have mood swings and bouts of depression? Do you have difficulty getting excited about what you do and staying motivated? Are you essentially a self-centered person who frequently talks about "me" to yourself and others and who primarily focuses on acquiring more material wealth? Are you uncertain what you want to be remembered for when you die? Do you sometimes ask yourself *"Is there more to life than this?"* Have you ever thought about suicide? Do you have mental health issues that prevent you from realizing your potential or that may require professional intervention?

IF YES: Approaching a job search with a clear sense of who you are and what you want to do will give you a major advantage over other candidates who may present a picture of uncertainty to prospective employers. You will appear centered and genuine throughout your interview. If you are a very self-centered and materialistic individual, your goals and purpose may relate to accumulating more financial resources for acquiring bigger and better toys and enjoying the finer material things in life. If you tend to be a spiritual individual, your purpose may relate to more humanistic and lofty goals. As you get older, your goals and purpose may shift more toward your family and personal legacy – the impact you want to have on others. You may want to reach out more to others, helping them through volunteerism and sharing your financial resources.

Purpose-driven individuals tend to have a clear sense of who they are and what they want to do in both their work and life. Other-directed, they tend to have positive outlook on life and exude a sense of self-confidence. They tend to be happy individuals who enjoy helping others. Self-motivated and centered, they know what they want to do and are focused on achieving goals.

TIPS: Employers want to hire focused individuals who have clear goals that are compatible with their operations. They look for purposeful, self-motivated, and genuine individuals who want to make a difference. They are suspicious of candidates who try to play them by giving answers the interviewee thinks the interviewer wants to hear. They look for, and often find, contradictions in the interviewee's answers to a variety of questions. Therefore, one of the first things you need to do before interviewing for a job is to **identify exactly what it is you want to do.** What do you most enjoy doing and really want to do in the future? What are your strengths? What motivates you to excel on your own? What are your short-, intermediate-, and long-term goals? If asked where you would like to be five years from now, what will you say? If asked about your legacy, how will you respond? You want to present a picture of a purposeful individual who has realistic goals and is self-assured and self-motivated.

Take the following quiz to determine to what degree you are a purpose-driven individual:

INSTRUCTIONS: Respond to each statement by circling which number at the right best represents your situation.

SCALE: 1 = Strongly agree
            2 = Agree
            3 = Maybe, not certain
            4 = Disagree
            5 = Strongly disagree

1. I know what I do well and enjoy doing.   1   2   3   4   5

2. I know what I want to achieve over the
   the next five years.   1   2   3   4   5

3. I have a written set of professional and
   personal goals that help guide me.   1   2   3   4   5

4. Within two minutes I can clearly explain
   my goals to a prospective employer.   1   2   3   4   5

5. I'm generally a very happy person.   1   2   3   4   5

6. I know what motivates me.   1   2   3   4   5

7. I have a clear sense of who I am and
   what I want to achieve in life.   1   2   3   4   5

8. I tend to be focused on what I do and
   am not easily distracted in getting
   things done.   1   2   3   4   5

9. I frequently volunteer my time and donate
   money to helping others.   1   2   3   4   5

10. I know what I want to be remembered for
    when I die.   1   2   3   4   5

Calculate your overall purpose-driven quotient by adding the numbers you circled for a composite score. If your total is more than 17 points, you may want to examine your goals and purpose. How you scored each item will indicate to what degree you need to work on changing your focus. If your score is under 15 points, you are probably a very purpose-driven and happy individual who should do well in presenting yourself to prospective employers!

The following books are good starting points for identifying your goals and purpose:

100 Ways to Motivate Yourself
Awaken the Giant Within
Dream It, Do It

Find Your Purpose, Change Your Life
Focal Point
Goals!
The Purpose-Driven Life
The Power of Purpose: Creating Meaning in Your Life and Work
The Power of Purpose: Living Well By Doing Good
The Purpose of Your Life
What Should I Do With the Rest of My Life?
Your Best Life Now
Your Leadership Legacy

If you occasionally have mood swings, experience bouts of depression, or appear distracted, you may want to seek professional help for what may be anything from a learning disability (ADD or ADHD) to a bipolar disorder to a substance abuse problem. Start by consulting these books, several of which include self-assessment exercises, before hiring a professional:

Bipolar Disorder
The Bipolar Disorder Survival Guide
Driven to Distraction
Feeling Good Handbook
Reinventing Your Life
Understanding Depression
You Mean I'm Not Lazy, Stupid, or Crazy?

TIP #8
Behave like a smart and productive farmer.

QUESTIONS: Do you often lack patience when engaged in difficult tasks? Do you tend to seek immediate gratification rather than postpone results? Do you get frustrated when you don't see quick results from your efforts? Do you have difficulty dealing with processes?

IF YES: You may have difficulty conducting a job search that could take you three to six months to connect with the right job. You may get frustrated and depressed when you don't see immediate results from your efforts. You also may have the urge to short-cut your job search by avoiding certain time-consuming activities that are key to getting job interviews and offers. For example, rather than spend three to four weeks conducting a self-assessment, researching different jobs and employers, and networking for information, advice, and referrals, many job seekers start their job search by writing a resume and then sending it to numerous employers in anticipation of quickly getting a job interview and offer. Neglecting the foundation activities of their job search that would focus on their strengths, such job seekers often enter the job market with a weak "obituary" resume that doesn't clearly communicate their goals, skills, and accomplishments to prospective employers. Lacking the patience to conduct a well organized job search centered on their strengths, they instead communicate their weaknesses to employers.

TIPS: It's best to view your job search as a form of smart farming – **you must take the necessary time and put in sufficient effort to plant the right seeds in order to later achieve a bountiful harvest.** Above all, you must be patient with this lengthy process. It requires good farming skills – knowing what you must do first, second, third, and fourth to make this process work. You must plant your seeds – start by conducting research and networking for information, advice, and referrals – and take care of them in an unpredictable environment in order to reap rewards. The whole process, which we might call the art of farming for a job, may take three to six months, depending on how patient and persistent you are in planting and nurturing your seeds.

TIP #9
Appear intellectually curious and capable.

QUESTIONS: Do you give definitive answers to most questions? Do you feel you know it all? When asked if you have any questions, do you usually respond by saying *"No"* or *"You've covered just about everything"*? During a job interview, do you primarily focus on yourself, what you will be expected to do, and your compensation? Do you feel uncomfortable in conversations that involve a free flow of ideas, with lots of give and take? Do you have difficulty giving examples of how you solved various problems and added value to an employer's operations? Do you avoid taking initiative?

IF YES: Interviewers and employers are attracted to individuals who are intelligent, thoughtful, curious, open-minded, take initiative, and are interesting to talk to and work with. They tend to be turned off by candidates who are highly opinionated and closed-minded, who fail to ask thoughtful questions about the job and company, who have difficulty giving examples of their capabilities, and who appear primarily motivated by salary and benefits. Such candidates appear to be unwilling to listen and learn from others. They lack self-motivation and self-direction and demonstrate few analytical abilities to solve problems. They most likely will need to be closely supervised and directed in order to achieve expected results. After all, one of the first things new employees need to do is to listen and learn in order to be effective in their new job.

TIPS: Intellectually curious individuals tend to be open-minded and ask thoughtful questions. Above all else, they are interested in learning about and from others. Indeed, they appear to be in a constant learning mode – trying to acquire more information and advice in order to make better decisions and do better work. They often respond to others' ideas by saying *"That's an interesting idea. What do you think about . . . ?"* Rather than focus on themselves and their job responsibilities, they focus on the job and employer as they try to learn more about what it is they can do to add value to the organization. If asked if they have any questions, their response is always *"Yes, I'm especially interested in learning more about . . ."* They then ask several questions that demonstrate their interest in the job and employer. In fact, the strongest stage of their interview is often this questioning period where they emphasize their interest and intelligence through the asking of questions. They ask compelling questions that make them very memorable. When it comes time to decide on which candidate to hire, the one that "asked very good questions" will often have the edge over others who appeared less curious about the job and employer.

Intellectually curious individuals are highly valued by organizations when they turn their intellectual curiosity into positive action. They demonstrate their ability to link learning to action when asked behavioral-based questions that focus on their decision-making style. Take, for example, this statement, which is a behavior-based question: *"Give me an example of a difficult problem you had to solve and did so to the surprise of others you worked with."* Intellectually curious and competent individuals who answer this question will focus on the information they acquired about the nature of the problem, how they defined the problem, and creative solutions to solving the problem, especially "thinking outside the box" solutions. Such a response demonstrates their capacity to learn and take appropriate actions.

Be prepared to ask several questions that demonstrate your intellectual curiosity. Avoid self-centered, canned, and stupid questions, such as *"What do you do here?,"* that do little to strengthen your candidacy. Ask inclusive behavior-based questions that make the interviewer think and reflect, such as *"Can you share with me some of your most recent strategies for improving market shares of product X? What was the thinking behind this decision? Who was involved in making the decision? If you had to do it over again, what changes would you make and why? Have you thought of perhaps benchmarking best practices found in last year's Extelor report?"* A candidate who asks a series of such questions appears both curious and knowledgeable. He is likely to be remembered as such when it comes time to make a hiring decision.

TIP #10
Become more extroverted in your approach
to meeting and conversing with strangers.

QUESTIONS: Do you feel uncomfortable meeting strangers, engaging in small talk, and sustaining conversations? Do you understand how to network but prefer not engaging in this activity? When invited to a party or social hour, do you feel uncomfortable mingling with others and keep an eye on your watch and the exit door? Would you rather be at home instead of attending meetings? Do you get nervous getting up in front of a group to speak? Are you generally a shy person who prefers staying in the background rather than standing out front?

IF YES: One of the biggest roadblocks to both job search and on-the-job success is the failure to network properly. Networking is especially easy for highly extroverted and socially active individuals, but many shy and introverted people simply avoid situations that would require them to meet strangers and strike up conversations. They don't know how to build, maintain, and expand networks of personal and professional relationships that are keys to success.

TIPS: If you are shy and introverted, you can still become an effective networker by learning some basic people skills that focus on building, maintaining, and expanding networks. These involve informational interviews, developing communication skills, and networking for information, advice, and referrals. Many job seekers have a clear understanding of the networking process – its central importance, how it works, and how to do it – but they fail to organize and implement an effective networking campaign. They may get started by contacting a few friends for information, advice, and referrals, but they soon fall back on old habits that seem less risky and more assuring – responding to classified ads with resumes and letters. Part of this reluctance to engage in an active networking campaign may go back to some cultural issues related to childhood – parental admonitions not to talk to strangers nor be too assertive or personal among friends. Many people also are reluctant to make cold calls because they fear encountering rejections. If these are issues preventing you from developing an effective networking campaign in your job search, we recommend the following books and audiotapes to help you develop the necessary skills and motivation to network:

Dig Your Well Before You're Thirsty
Endless Referrals
Fine Art of Small Talk
A Foot in the Door
How to Work a Room
The Little Black Book of Connections
Make Your Contacts Count
Masters of Networking
Networking for Job and Career Success
Networking Smart
Never Eat Alone
One Phone Call Away
Power Networking
The Power to Get In
The Savvy Networker
Work the Pond

The following websites also provide a wealth of information on the networking process for job seekers:

- WetFeet   www.wetfeet.com/advice/networking.asp
- Monster.com   http://network.monster.com

- **Quintessential Careers**   www.quintcareers.com/network ing.html
- **Riley Guide**   www.rileyguide.com/netintv.html
- **About.com**   http://about.com/humanresources/ networking
- **Susan RoAne**   www.susanroane.com/free.html
- **Contacts Count**   www.contactscount.com

5

You Mean There's More Than One?

M OST CANDIDATES PREPARE for one type of interview – a traditional interview that may involve scores of standard questions. Viewing the job interview as basically a question/ answer session, they try to learn the questions most frequently asked by interviewers as well as develop appropriate responses that will impress the interviewer. In other words, they learn to play the role of the "good interviewee" whose goal is to ace the interview and get the job offer. Accordingly, they find comfort in reading one or more of these popular question/answer job interview books as part of their job search preparation:

101 Great Answers to the Toughest Interview Questions
101 Toughest Interview Questions . . . and Answers That Win the Job
250 Job Interview Questions You'll Most Likely Be Asked . . . and the Answers That Will Get You Hired!
301 Smart Answers to Tough Interview Questions
501+ Great Interview Questions for Employers and the Best Answers for Prospective Employees
Best Answers to the 201 Most Frequently Asked Interview Questions

Complete Q&A Job Interview Book
The Everything Practice Interview Book
*More Best Answers to the 201 Most Frequently Asked
    Interview Questions*
*Nail the Job Interview: 101 Dynamite Answers to Interview
    Questions*

If you follow the advice of these books, you should be able to lessen your interview anxiety by being well prepared to answer many standard interview questions.

Traditional Interview Questions and Hiring

While most such books do a good job in preparing candidates for the rich variety of questions asked at a job interview, they only help prepare interviewees for certain types of interviews. They typically focus on a traditional interview which involves such standard questions as:

- *Tell me about yourself.*
- *What did you enjoy the most/least about your last job?*
- *What are some of your major weaknesses/strengths?*
- *Where do you see yourself five years from now?*
- *How would your supervisor/co-workers describe you?*
- *Why are you looking for another job?*
- *Why did you decide to major in _____ at XYZ University?*
- *How well do you work under pressure?*
- *Describe your typical workday.*
- *Why should we hire you?*

Employers who conduct a traditional interview using such questions tend to look for indirect personality and behavioral cues rather than direct indicators of job performance, which are the focus of behavioral and situational interviews. In fact, most traditional interview questions have little or nothing to do with work-related competencies but a lot to do with personality, communication, and likability. In the end, employers who screen candidates based on such questions tend to make an educated guess as to which candidate can best do the job and, accordingly, hire the individual they like the most. Accepting the fact that hiring is a risky business, employers tend to trust their gut – they have a good feeling they are making the right hiring decision. **Likability**, rather than objective measures or indicators of performance or "fit," becomes the central consideration in making such a hiring decision.

If you want to prepare well for such interviews, we recommend that you do what many other interviewees do in preparation for the job interview – consult the many sample question/answer books listed on pages 51 and 52. However, you may still be in for some surprises that are not revealed in such books, especially when you feel unprepared for other types of questions and exercises you encounter. Indeed, you may express the lament of job seekers who were unprepared for multiple interviews, brain teaser questions, psychological tests, and a barrage of difficult questions related to behavioral and situational interviews – *"I can't believe they asked me that!"* In the end, you

> *Most traditional interview questions have little to do with work-related competencies but a lot to do with personality, communication, and likability.*

may wish you had prepared for the job interview by following the many tips outlined in this book rather than trying to play the "good interviewee" role by practicing best answers to expected interview questions!

Different Types of Interviews

Employers conduct many different types of interviews to determine if candidates are the right fit for their company or organization. Let's examine the eight most frequently encountered types. Our first five interview types relate to the **interview setting**. The final three types focus on **questioning techniques**. The most common types of interviews include:

1. **One-on-one interviews:** This is the traditional entry-level type of interview most job seekers expect – meeting and exchanging information with one individual, the interviewer or employer. This usually takes place at the employer's office where the candidate and employer sit down to discuss the position and the applicant's skills, knowledge, and abilities.

2 **Sequential interviews:** These are a series of interviews with candidates being screened in or out after each interview. With sequential interviews, many employment issues such as salary and benefits may not be discussed in the initial interview. These interviews can work to your advantage – with each interview you should have the opportunity to find out more about the position and ask questions you forgot to bring up in previous interviews.

3. **Serial interviews:** These consist of several interviews, one after the other. Usually each meeting is with a different person or group of people within the organization, and all the interviews will be held over a one- or two-day period. Following these interviews, the interviewers will meet to compare notes and make a group hiring decision.

4. **Panel interviews:** These interviews occur infrequently, but you may encounter them. In a panel interview you are interviewed by several people at the same time. These are among the most stressful interview situations. At its best, you are facing several people at the same time, responding to the questions of one panel member as you try to balance your perceptions of the other members' expectations.

5. **Group interviews:** On occasion you may encounter this type of competitive interview. Here you find yourself being interviewed along with several other applicants. In group interviews the employer will observe the interpersonal skills of the applicants. Often a question will be posed to the group, or the group will be presented with a problem to solve. At least you'll know your competition when placed in such an interview setting!

6. **Behavioral interviews:** Behavioral interviews are based on the simple and commonsense notion that the **best predictor of present and future performance is knowledge of past patterns of behavior.** The interviewer's task is to either understand or observe the **actual behavior** of candidates in relationship to the position in question. Many employers like to use

behavioral interviews because they probe the thought processes and decision-making skills of candidates. Best of all, they know individuals cannot prepare well for such interviews. Variations of this type of interview include competency-based interview questions and brainteaser questions.

Competency-based interview questions focus on the specific competencies required for performing the job. Interviewers carefully structure questions, which they believe are good indicators of specific required competencies relevant to the position.

Popularized by Microsoft, **brainteaser questions** such as _"Why are manhole covers round?"_ or _"How many Starbucks are in China?"_ attempt to examine analytical, problem-solving, and decision-making capabilities along with intelligence.

> _Many employers prefer conducting behavioral interviews because they know individuals cannot prepare well for such interviews._

Behavior-based interviews usually involve self-appraisal questions, situational questions, and hypothetical situational questions. For example, an interviewer might ask, _"In what situations have you become so involved in the work you were doing that the day flew by?"_ If you have been explaining how you handled an irate customer, the interviewer might ask, _"If you were to encounter that same situation now, how would you deal with that customer?"_ Situation questions might include _"Tell me about a recent time when you took responsibility for a task that was outside of your job description."_ Hypothetical situational questions ask the applicant what he would do in a hypothetical situation. Thus they give the interviewer the opportunity to ask questions about situations the applicant may never have actually encountered in a previous position. For information about these types of interviews, including many sample questions, see the following interview books:

High-Impact Interview Questions: 701 Behavior-Based
Questions to Find the Right Person for Every Job
Preparing for the Behavior-Based Interview
Competency-Based Interviews

7. **Examination/test interviews:** Some interviews will include elements of testing or examination. For some types of jobs, such as clerical or mechanical, you may be tested on the actual equipment you will be using. For example, if a job requires a high level of keyboard proficiency, and if you claim you can keyboard 80 words a minute with a high degree of accuracy, be prepared to have your claims tested as part of the interview – in fact, you will probably be asked to show off your keyboard skills through a 10-minute typing exercise. A school or university that requires excellent classroom skills may ask prospective teachers to conduct a one-hour classroom session where their performance will be observed and evaluated by both faculty and students. In such interviews, certain questions may be asked to ascertain your level of knowledge, decision-making capabilities, analytic capabilities, and competence. *"What if"* questions that begin with *"What would you do if . . ."* are designed to test your ability to relate your past experience to the employer's current situation and needs. Using questions designed to test you, interviewers are looking for thoughtful answers that demonstrate your competence.

8. **Situational interviews:** If you watched the popular television program "The Apprentice," you probably know what an extensive situational interview is all about. Over a period of several weeks prospective job candidates undergo intensive scrutiny by both employers and fellow team members to demonstrate their decision-making capabilities and entrepreneurial skills – key indicators of their ability to perform well in a coveted job. While this is an extreme case of a situational interview, nonetheless, more and more employers are using these interviews to screen the **actual observed performance** of candidates. In a situational interview, a candidate is asked to deal with an actual work-related situation or problem where he or she can be

observed making decisions and generating positive or negative outcomes. For example, if you are interviewing for a customer service position, you might be asked to handle a telephone call from an irate customer. You'll be observed trying to solve the customer's problem. How well you handle that customer may determine whether or not you will be offered the job. Like the behavioral interview, it's difficult to prepare for such interviews. Indeed, employers like these interviews because they can observe the actual behavior of candidates solving problems they will likely encounter on a day-to-day basis.

Psychological and Other Tests

Psychological testing is playing an increasingly important role in today's hiring process. It's used to probe for red flags that might not be evident through other screening techniques. Indeed, think of employment screening tests as pseudo-scientific **red flag catchers**. Since employers want to better predict the future performance of candidates beyond mere educated guesses, gut reactions, or fortune telling, they try to use various assessment instruments that claim to have predictive power. Some employers require interviewees to take psychological tests in order to determine whether or not they have the right personality for the job. Much of this testing is based upon the *Myers-Briggs Type Indicator®* (MBTI), which attempts to measure personality dispositions and interests – the way people absorb information, decide, and communicate. The MBTI analyzes preferences to four dichotomies (extroversion/introversion, sensing/intuiting, thinking/feeling, judging/perceiving) which result in 16 personality types. Candidates interviewing for sales positions, which require specific types of extroverted personalities, may be asked to take psychological tests as part of the interview process. Employers who have a clear understanding of the type of personality that is best suited for a position may want candidates to take such psychological tests before hiring them. Employers using such tests usually set pass/fail criteria for screening candidates.

> *Psychological testing is increasingly used by employers to probe for red flags that might not be evident through other screening techniques.*

Candidates also may encounter other types of tests that attempt to measure their intelligence, their ability to analyze problems, or their degree of honesty or deception. After all, employers don't want to hire individuals who have difficulty making decisions, taking initiative, telling the truth, or who are otherwise psychologically challenged. Indeed, this type of testing has become a big business in recent years. Companies that develop and administer such instruments suggest that the results of these tests are much better predictors of future performance of candidates than most traditional interview questioning techniques. Whether or not they actually do predict according to such claims is another question altogether. In the end, these tests give employers additional pieces of useful information to include in their hiring decisions. If, for example, the interviewee appears to be very honest, forthcoming, and entrepreneurial in the job interview but test results indicate a possible high level of deception and an introverted personality, an employer would be well advised to do a very extensive background check on the candidate to validate the test results as well as shift the focus of the interview to more behavioral- and situational-type interview questions. If such tests seem to contradict other information on the candidate, an employer should pass on this person or be prepared to encounter on-the-job problems.

At the same time, such testing raises serious questions about privacy and ethics. Many candidates, as well as lawyers, feel such testing is an illegal invasion of their privacy and potentially very discriminatory, especially when they raise questions about the reliability and validity of assessment instruments. For example, some people who are impeccably honest simply cannot pass tests that probe for deception. They literally flunk polygraph tests! Should such people automatically be eliminated from consideration because of such testing results? As many seasoned professionals will admit, psychological testing has real limitations and thus should not be relied upon too much in the hiring process.

For information on different types of personality inventories and other employment-related tests, see the following books:

Aptitude, Personality, and Motivation Tests
Career Tests
Gifts Differing
Quick Guide to the 16 Personality Types in Organizations
Type Talk At Work

The Ultimate Book of Personality Tests
What's Your Type of Career?
What Type Am I?
Who Do You Think You Are?

Increasing Number of Interviews

Don't expect to get hired based upon a single interview with an employer. Indeed, more and more employers are subjecting candidates to a series of interviews these days. Each interview may involve a different level of questioning and examination. For example, the first interview may follow more traditional lines – a one-on-one interview that attempts to determine whether or not you are liked enough to invite you to a second interview. The second interview may involve meeting more people in the organization and a series of behavioral interview questions. The third interview may be with key decision-makers and involve very targeted competency-based behavioral questions. A fourth interview may encompass even more in-depth interview questions as well as a battery of psychological and/or aptitude tests. The fifth interview may result in a job offer followed by salary negotiations. Some candidates report seven or eight interviews with a single employer. Therefore, don't be surprised if this whole process takes a great deal of time and involves multiple interviews.

TIP #11
Anticipate and prepare for questions.

QUESTIONS: Are you uncertain what you will be asked during the job interview? Do you get nervous at the thought of having to spend an hour with a stranger answering questions about your skills and abilities? Do you feel there is not much you can do other than just show up and answer questions?

IF YES: You can anticipate before you even walk into the interview 90-95 percent of the questions you will be asked. You can expect to be asked about your education and work experience as they relate to the job under consideration. You may be asked questions about your personality, work habits, ability to work with others, or your career goals. In addition to the standard areas of inquiry, a look at your resume should tell you if there are areas likely to get the attention of the interviewer. Do you have red flags showing, such as unexplained time gaps in your education or work life? Have you jumped around from employer to employer in a short time period? Are you applying for a position that is significantly below your apparent abilities and previous work experience?

TIPS: Since you will be showcasing your best behavior in the job interview, **always anticipate and thoroughly prepare for possible questions.** You can do this by examining the many lists of possible questions outlined by interview experts, preparing a strategy for answering each question, practicing the actual interview scenario to determine how well you answer various questions, and developing the best possible answers to each question. Be sure to focus on both your verbal and nonverbal behaviors during the interview. Develop a compelling two-minute pitch that addresses this key question – *"Why should I hire you?"*

TIP #12
Prepare as if you were about to win a
$1 million+ prize for being the best!

QUESTIONS: Do you think that getting a job offer is primarily a function of luck? Do you believe there is not much you can do to influence the outcome of a job interview? Is getting a job offer similar to winning the lottery? Are you planning to just "wing it" at the job interview?

IF YES: If you believe you can't do much to influence the outcome of a job interview, you probably won't be well prepared to deal with each stage of the job interview. Indeed, you may not even pass the first five minutes of the interview where initial impressions count the most! You will appear unprepared and thus unworthy of the job. After all, employers expect you to put your best foot forward in the job interview. They expect you to come well prepared. If you're not prepared, you send an important negative message to a prospective employer – he or she was not important enough for you to spend some time getting prepared for this meeting. Furthermore, you will probably treat your job in a similar manner – always unprepared and taking little initiative to produce results. Like an actor on stage, you have an important role to play in the interview – the interviewee – and that role requires good preparation in order to deliver a flawless performance.

TIPS: Treat the job interview as a form of competition that results in a $1 million+ prize for the winner. While in most cases you don't know who your competition is, rest assured you are up against competition that may be better prepared for the interview than you. After all, landing this job could result in more than $1 million in additional income during the next 20 years. There's a great deal of truth to the old saying that the best qualified individuals doesn't necessarily get the job – only the person who is best prepared for the interview.

TIP #13
Use both print and online resources to prepare for the job interview.

QUESTIONS: Are you uncertain how to best prepare for the job interview? Do you need help in identifying possible interview questions and appropriate responses?

IF YES: You'll find a wealth of resources available to assist you with all phases of the job interview. Most of these resources are books and websites that focus on either the job search or job interview

TIPS: If you need help in preparing for the job interview, we recommend the following print and Internet resources:

Books

101 Dynamite Questions to Ask at Your Job Interview
101 Great Answers to the Toughest Interview Questions
250 Job Interview Questions You'll Most Likely Be Asked
301 Smart Answers to Tough Interview Questions
Adams Job Interview Almanac, with CD-ROM
Boost Your Interview I.Q.
Don't Blow the Interview
Haldane's Best Answers to Tough Interview Questions
Interview for Success
Interview Kit

Interview Magic
Interview Rehearsal Book
Job Interview Tips for People With Not-So-Hot Backgrounds
Job Interviews for Dummies
KeyWords to Nail Your Job Interview
Nail the Job Interview!
Naked at the Interview
Power Interviews
Preparing for the Behavior-Based Interview
Savvy Interviewing
Sweaty Palms
Winning the Interview Game
Winning Job Interviews

Websites

- Monster.com — www.interview.monster.com
- About.com — http://about.com/jobsearch/interview resources
- InterviewPro — www.interviewpro.com
- JobInterview.net — www.job-interview.net
- Interview Coach — www.interviewcoach.com
- Quintessential Careers — www.quintcareers.com/intvres.html
- Wetfeet.com — www.wetfeet.com/advice/interviewing.asp
- The Riley Guide — www.rileyguide.com/interview.interview.html
- Jobweb — www.jobweb.com/Resumes_Interviews_default.htm
- WSACorp.com — www.WSACorp.com

TIP #14
Approach the interview as an important information exchange.

QUESTIONS: Do you view the job interview as a form of gamesmanship – consisting of winners and losers? Do you believe the main purpose of the job interview is to get a job offer? Do you try to "score points" as you progress through the job interview?

IF YES: Most people still view interview success in narrow terms: success is to get a job offer. But to get the job offer is only one of many outcomes of the employment interview which may or may not be positive for you. Only time and experience on the job will tell you if getting the job was a good idea.

TIPS: An important goal and outcome of any job interview should be to **obtain useful information** to determine whether the job is right for you. Success in the interview may mean learning that the position is **not** for you, and thus you turn down the job offer. Or perhaps the offer is not made since the interviewer also realizes the job is not a good fit for you. If you view a major goal of your interview to be gathering information, you will most likely perform better in the interview situation. Rather than feel you are in a stressful win-lose game, you will be more at ease as you focus on what the interview is all about – **an exchange of useful information between the interviewer and interviewee.** It is to your advantage to make sure this exchange takes place in your favor. You gain information about the job and present yourself, with honesty, in the most positive way possible.

Another successful outcome would be to market yourself for future positions in this or other organizations. The interview could establish a good basis for developing a job information and referral network.

We urge you to approach the interview as a two-way street: both you and the employer want to better know each other. While the interviewer is trying to determine whether to hire you, you should be determining whether you want to work for the employer. There is nothing worse than dampening the euphoria of getting the job with the realization two months later that the job is not right for you. So beware of supposedly positive outcomes – job offers – that can lead to negative career experiences!

TIP #15
Join or form a support group.

QUESTIONS: Do you plan to conduct a job search on your own? Are you reluctant to talk to others about your job search experiences? Will you prepare for the job interview by yourself?

IF YES: Finding a job is often a lonely and frustrating experience if you do it on your own. However, you can significantly improve the effectiveness of your job search, as well as shorten your job search time, by involving others in your job search. Involve your family, friends, and others who are interested in conducting a job search. If you're married, your spouse should become a member of your support group.

Job clubs are designed to provide a group structure and support system to individuals seeking employment. These groups typically consist of about 12 individuals who are led by a trained counselor and supported with computers, telephones, copying machines, and a resource center. Formal job clubs, such as the 40-Plus Clubs (www.40plus.org/chapters) and the Five O'Clock Clubs (www.fiveoclockclub.com), organize job search activities for both the advertised and hidden job markets. Job club activities may include:

- Signing commitment agreements to achieve specific job search goals and targets.

- Contacting friends, relatives, and acquaintances for job leads.

- Completing activity forms.

- Using telephones, computers, photocopy machines, postage, and other equipment and supplies.

- Meeting with fellow participants to discuss job search progress.

- Meeting with career counselors or other career specialists.

- Attending job fairs and hiring conferences.

- Telephoning to uncover job leads.

- Using the Internet to research the job market and contact potential employers.

- Researching newspapers, telephone books, and directories.

- Developing research, telephone, interview, and social skills.

- Writing letters and resumes.

- Responding to employment ads.

- Completing employment applications.

- Assessing weekly progress and sharing information with fellow group members.

In other words, the job club formalizes many of the prospecting, networking, and informational interviewing activities within a group context and interjects the role of the telephone as the key communication device for developing and expanding networks.

Many job clubs place excessive reliance on using the telephone and Internet for uncovering job leads. Members call prospective employers and ask about job openings. The Yellow Pages and the Internet become the job hunter's best friends. During a two-week period, a job club member might spend most of his or her mornings telephoning for job leads and scheduling interviews. Afternoons are normally devoted to job interviewing.

Many job club methods are designed for individuals who need a job – any job – quickly. Since individuals try to fit into available vacancies, their specific objectives and skills are of secondary concern. Other job club methods are more consistent with the focus and methods outlined in this book, especially those used by 40-Plus Clubs and Five O'Clock Clubs.

TIPS: In lieu of participating in such clubs, you may want to form your own **support group** that adapts some job club methods around our central concept of finding a job fit for you – one appropriate to your objective and in line with your particular mix of skills, abilities, and interests. Support groups are a useful alternative to job clubs. They have one major advantage over conducting a job search on your own: they may cut your job search time in half because they provide an important structure for achieving goals. Forming or joining one of these groups can help direct as well as enhance your individual job search activities.

Your support group should consist of three or more individuals who are job hunting. Try to schedule regular meetings with specific purposes in mind. While the group may be highly social, especially if it involves close friends, it also should be **task-oriented**. Meet at least once a week and include your spouse. At each meeting set **performance goals** for the week. For example, your goal can be to make 20 new contacts and conduct five informational interviews. The contacts can be made by telephone, e-mail, letter, or in person. Share your experiences and job information with each other. **Critique** each other's progress, make suggestions for improving the job search, and develop new strategies together. By doing this, you will be gaining valuable information and feedback which is normally difficult to gain on your own. This group should provide important psychological supports to help you through your job search. After all, job hunting can be a lonely, frustrating, and exasperating experience. By sharing your experiences with others, you will find you are not alone. You will quickly learn that rejections are part of the game. The group will encourage you, and you will feel good about helping others achieve their goals. Try building small incentives into the group, such as the individual who receives the most job interviews for the month will be treated to dinner by other members of the group.

> *Job hunting can be a lonely, frustrating, and exasperating experience. Sharing your experiences with a support group can provide important psychological supports to help you through your job search.*

This group can be especially helpful in preparing you for the job interview. You can role play with members, who can give you useful feedback on how well you performed in a mock interview and suggestions on how you can improve your performance.

TIP #16
Practice the job interview with a mirror,
tape recorder, camera, and others.

QUESTIONS: Are you uncertain how to practice the job interview? Do you plan to primarily read books and articles on how to interview?

IF YES: While reading to understand how to best interview for a job is useful, it's no substitute for engaging in a mock interview where you actually play the role of the interviewee. Indeed, the best interview preparation is to practice answering and asking questions you are likely to be asked at the interview. You need to engage in an interview and get feedback on your performance in order to perfect your interview skills.

TIPS: We highly recommend getting dressed for an interview and then stand in front of a full-length mirror to examine yourself from head to toe. How do you look? Are you appropriately attired for the job interview and position in question? If you are practicing the interview by yourself, tape record your answers and questions. How do you sound? Do you speak in complete sentences and avoid vocalized pauses? Do you sound enthusiastic and energetic? Do you ask thoughtful questions that will impress the interviewer? If you are working with others in doing a mock interview, try to film the interview. Replay the video and ask others to critique both your verbal and nonverbal behavior and grade yourself on a scale of 0 to 10. Practice the interview scenario again and again until you can give yourself a perfect 10.

TIP #17
Don't try to memorize answers to questions.

QUESTIONS: Do you try to memorize answers to anticipated interview questions? Do you have difficulty answering open-ended questions? Do you know how to communicate energy, enthusiasm, and interest during the job interview?

IF YES: Unless you are an extremely good actor, people who memorize interview scripts will tend to be nervous, lack spontaneity and enthusiasm, communicate a lack of authenticity, focus on themselves, and offer canned answers. Worst of all, they may appear dishonest because their verbal and nonverbal behaviors may be at odds with each other as they try to deliver memorized lines. When they forget or stumble over their lines, they create awkward and unforgiving situations that raise questions about their trustworthiness.

Remember, employers want to discover the real you – not encounter an individual who tries to be someone he or she is not. If an employer asks you behavioral or situational questions, which require you to think on your feet, you will most likely have trouble answering such questions because you only prepared to give canned answers to traditional interview questions. It won't be long before an interviewer recognizes the fact that you came to the interview to deliver interview scripts rather than discuss what you have done, can do, and will do for him. Suspicious that he may be dealing with someone who is less than genuine and forthcoming, he may quickly conclude with a gut reaction that there is "something wrong" about this candidate – it just doesn't feel right. Unable to build trust during the interview, you will probably be eliminated from further consideration.

Few people are really good actors who can flawlessly play roles and deliver scripts. Whatever you do, don't go the direction of memorizing answers to interview questions. If you do, you may quickly flunk your audition.

TIPS: While it's important to a develop answers to anticipated interview questions, you should never attempt to develop scripts and memorize answers. Instead, develop **strategies and approaches** for answering different types of questions. Focus on how you might best approach a question. For example, do you use positive language? Do you give thoughtful answers that go beyond a quick *"yes"* or *"no"*? Does the content of your answers focus on the needs of the employer (employer-centered) rather than on your needs (self-centered)? Do you use inclusive language such as *"we"* or *"us"* rather than *"me"* or *"I"*? Can you give examples of your accomplishments, especially problems you solved with previous employers? Is the content of your answers, as well as your questions, both interesting and enthusiastic? Do you appear interested in both the job and the employer? If you focus only on developing and delivering an interview script, you will overlook the most important qualities employers look for in the question/answer format of a job interview.

TIP #18
Prepare to deal with sensitive and illegal questions.

QUESTIONS: Are you uncertain how you would deal with a sensitive or illegal question during the interview? Are you unclear about your legal rights when interviewing for a job?

IF YES: Title VII of the Civil Rights Act of 1964 makes discrimination on the basis of race, sex, religion, or national origins illegal in personnel decisions. The Americans With Disabilities Act of 1990 includes questions related to disabilities as being illegal. Questions that delve into these areas as well as others, such as age, height, or weight, are illegal, unless they can be shown to directly relate to bona fide occupational qualifications. If a question relates directly to the job, it is usually legal to ask.

Most interviewers are well aware of these restrictions and will not ask you illegal questions. However, you may still encounter such questions either because of ignorance on the part of the interviewer or blatant violation of the regulations. Many interviewers may ask these questions indirectly. However, some interviewers still ask them directly.

Women are more likely to face illegal questions than men. Some employers still ask questions regarding birth control, child care, or how their husbands feel about them working or traveling. The following types of questions are considered illegal:

- *Are you married, divorced, separated, single, or gay?*
- *How old are you?*
- *Do you go to church regularly?*
- *Do you have many debts?*
- *How many children do you have?*
- *Do you own or rent your home?*
- *What social or political organizations do you belong to?*
- *What does your spouse think about your career?*
- *Are you living with anyone?*
- *Are you practicing birth control?*
- *Were you ever arrested?*
- *What kind of insurance do you carry?*
- *How much do you weigh?*
- *How tall are you?*

- *Do you have any particular disabilities?*
- *What do your parents do?*
- *Have you ever been treated for depression?*
- *Do you ever been diagnosed with ADHD?*
- *Have you ever sued an employer or co-worker?*
- *How often do you see a doctor?*
- *Have you had any mental health or psychiatric problems?*

TIPS: Consider the following options for handling illegal and personal questions. If you encounter such questions, your choice may depend upon which is more important to you: defending a principle or giving yourself the greatest chance to land the job. You may decide the job is not as important as the principle. Or you may decide, even though you really want this job, you could never work in an organization that employed such clods, and tell them so.

On the other hand, you may choose to answer the question, offensive though it may be, because you really want the job. If you get the job, you vow you will work from within the organization to change such interview practices.

There is yet a third scenario here. You may believe the employer is purposefully trying to see how you will react to stressful questions. Will you lose your temper or will you answer meekly? Though a rather dangerous practice for employers, this does occur. In this situation you should remain cool and answer tactfully by indicating indirectly that the questions may be inappropriate.

For example, if you are divorced and the interviewer asks about your divorce, you could respond by asking, *"Does a divorce have a direct bearing on the responsibilities of this position?"*

A possible response to any illegal question – regardless of motive – is to turn what appears to be a negative into a positive. If, for example, you are female and the interviewer asks you how many children you still have living at home and you say, *"I have five – two boys and three girls,"* you can expect this one-sentence answer will be viewed as a negative. Working mothers with five children at home may be viewed as neither good mothers nor dependable employees. Therefore, you could immediately follow this response with a tactful elaboration that will turn this potential negative into a positive. You might say,

I have five – two boys and three girls. They are wonderful children who, along with my understanding husband, take great care of each other. If I didn't have such a supportive and caring family, I would never think of pursuing a career in this field. I do want you to know that I keep my personal life separate from my professional life. That's very important to me and my family, and I know it's important to employers. In fact, because of my family situation, I make special arrangements with other family members, friends, and day-care centers to ensure that family responsibilities never interfere with my work. But, more important, I think being a mother and working full time has really given me a greater sense of responsibility, forced me to use my time well, and helped me better organize my life and handle stress. I've learned what's important in both my work and life. I would hope that the fact that I'm both a mother and I'm working – and not a working mother – would be something your company would be supportive of, especially given my past performance and the qualifications I would bring to this job.

TIP #19
Prepare to tell your story in reference
to the employer's hiring needs.

QUESTIONS: When asked to tell an interviewer about yourself, do you tend to focus on a chronology of your personal and/or work history? Do you have difficulty talking about yourself to others? Do you need to prepare a set of stories about yourself that clearly emphasizes your major skills, abilities, and accomplishments?

IF YES: One of the best ways to prepare for a job interview is to put together several stories about yourself. Like illustrations and examples, stories are one of the most effective ways to make points and be remembered by employers, especially when your stories relate to the needs of the employer. Indeed, individuals with strong story-telling skills have a distinct advantage in job interviews. They know how to tell compelling stories about their accomplishments in reference to the employer's needs. They are adept at telling and re-telling stories about what they have done, can do, and will do in the future. Individuals who do not understand importance of stories and thus are unprepared to tell stories may wa aimlessly when encountering one of the most frequently asked opening questions: *"Tell me about yourself."* Employers who ask these questions are not really interested in learning about your personal or professional history, which is already outlined on your resume. They want you to tell them about your **skills, abilities, and accomplishments** as they may relate to the position in question.

TIPS: Ask yourself what are the five most memorable stories about your accomplishments that will likely impress potential employers? Your stories should focus on your skills, abilities, and accomplishments. Try to develop five different one- to three-minute stories in which you focus on what you have done, can do, and will do in the future – the three major concerns of employers. If you are well prepared, you might take three minutes to tell your story – talk about your major strengths and patterns of accomplishments as they relate to the needs of the employer. For example, if you are interviewing for a marketing position, your story should focus on marketing experiences that resulted in positive outcomes for previous employers. Try to include challenging situations that resulted in outcomes measured in percentage or dollar figures. Instead of telling a prospective employer that you graduated from XYZ university with a B.A. in psychology, tell the interviewer why you decided to study psychology and how it relates to your career goals, including the job for which you are interviewing.

These two books can help you develop some great stories for preparing for the job interview:

The Story of You: And How to Create a New One
Tell Your Story, Win the Job

TIP #20
Expect to encounter behavioral interviews.

QUESTIONS: Are you uncertain how to prepare for a behavioral interview? Do you have difficulty giving examples of your accomplishments? Are you nervous about answering hypothetical questions?

IF YES: More and more employers conduct behavioral interviews because they feel they get more accurate and candid information from candidates using behavioral questioning techniques. They also know most candidates do not prepare for these interviews and thus are least likely to engage in role playing. Interviewers who conduct behavioral interviews typically ask open-ended self-appraisal, situational, and hypothetical situational questions that require candidates to think on their feet and give examples of their behaviors and experiences. For example, they often ask questions that start as follows:

Tell me about a situation....
Tell me about a time....
Give me an example....
Describe an occasion....
Describe a work situation....
Think about a time when....
Share with me your experience....

These questions require interviewees to quickly come up with real-life examples of their performance and formulate them into coherent stories.

TIPS: While it is more difficult to prepare for behavioral interviews, because you don't know exactly what you might be asked, nonetheless, you can and should prepare for such interviews. The best way to do this is to develop numerous **examples** related to a variety of behavioral topics, such as your analytical skills, dealing with ambiguity, managing conflict, cooperating, teamwork, decision making, customer relations, goal setting, using humor, taking initiative, motivating self and others, negotiating, tenacity, problem solving, risk taking, handling stress, managing time, making and correcting mistakes, listening, delegating, initiating change, and handling conflicts. A good starting point in preparation for such interviews are these three books:

Competency-Based Interviews
High-Impact Interview Questions: 701 Behavior-Based
    Questions to Find the Right Person for Every Job
Preparing for the Behavior-Based Interview

Individuals with strong story-telling skills, as we indicated in Tip #18, should be able to handle such interviews with ease.

TIP #21
Prepare for different questioning techniques.

QUESTIONS: Do you have difficulty identifying different questioning techniques? Do you sometimes loose your cool under stress?

IF YES: While you may be prepared to respond to direct questions with direct answers, some interviewers also include indirect and stress questioning techniques. For example, rather than ask *"Do you have difficulty working with your employers?,"* they may ask *"Why did you leave your last three jobs?"* or *"How did you get along with your last three employers?"* Rather than ask you directly about your social status and financial situation, they may ask *"Where do you prefer living in the community?"* If a job involves a great deal of stress, the interviewer may ask you questions that put you under stress during the interview just to see how you handle such situations. For example, you may unexpectedly be asked *"If we hire you and three months later decide you're not the person we want, what are we going to do?"* or *"We normally don't hire someone without a college degree. Do you plan to complete college?"* You may very well be thrown questions that are designed to challenge what may be perceived to be your well-rehearsed interview script. Remember, interviewers will be looking for indications of your weaknesses by asking questions that elicit such indicators.

TIPS: Develop a strategy for responding to indirect and stress questions. Keep focused on communicating your strengths – skills, abilities, and accomplishments – rather than on revealing weaknesses

TIP #22
Know how to communicate verbally to others.

QUESTIONS: Do you sometimes have difficulty answering questions in clear and coherent sentences? Do you need to improve your diction and grammar? Are you often tentative in answering questions? Do you use negative terms when talking about others?

IF YES: Strong verbal communication skills are highly valued by most employers. They are signs of educated and competent individuals. Do you, for example, speak in complete and intelligible sentences? How is your diction? Do you say *"going"* rather than *"goin',"* *"going to"* rather than *"gonna,"* *"didn't"* rather than *"din't,"* *"yes"* rather than *"yea"*? Do you have a tendency to use vocalized phases (*"ah"* and *"uhm"*) and fillers (*"you know,"* *"like,"* *"okay"*)? How is your grammar? Do you use the active rather than passive voice? Do you avoid using tentative, indecisive terms, such as *"I think,"* *"I guess,"* *"I feel"*? Do you avoid ambiguous and negative terms such as *"pretty good"* or *"fairly well"* which say little if anything? They may even communicate negatives – that what you did was not good!

TIPS: If you plan for the job interview on your own, tape record answers to various interview questions and then listen to your answers for possible red flags. Evaluate your performance by asking questions about your sentence structure, diction, grammar, vocalized phases, fillers, decisiveness, and use of negative terms. If you are working with someone else, also have them evaluate your performance.

TIP #23
Know how to communicate nonverbally to others.

QUESTIONS: Do you need to sharpen your nonverbal communication skills? Are you uncertain what messages you convey when you shake hands, smile, and eat?

IF YES: Over 80 percent of what you communicate in the interview is nonverbal. Indeed, as soon as you enter the door, shake hands, sit down in the chair, and engage in small talk – usually the first five minutes of the interview – the interviewer has already made up his mind whether or not he likes you. Most of the information being communicated at this point is nonverbal – your appearance, demeanor, smell, feel, facial expressions, and eye contact. If he doesn't initially like you, the remainder of the interview will be a waste of his time. Indeed, you may find the interview will go very fast and you'll be thanked for coming as he closes the interview for good.

So how do you dress, groom, greet, shake hands, use eye contact, sit, maintain posture, use your hands, move your head, maintain facial expressions, listen positively, eat, drink, or enter and leave a room? These are nonverbal behaviors that may communicate more about your competence and personality than what you say in the interview.

TIPS: You may want to videotape yourself in a mock interview to see how well you communicate both verbally and nonverbally. You need to work with two people – someone who can play the role of the interviewer and someone who can observe your nonverbal interview behavior. Pay particular attention to the nonverbal aspects of your encounter – your appearance and how you initially greet the interviewer, eye contact, listening behavior, and interview close. For a complete examination of nonverbal behaviors in the job interview, see Caryl and Ron Krannich's *The Savvy Interviewer: The Nonverbal Advantage*.

TIP #24
Prepare to dress appropriately for the job interview.

QUESTIONS: Are you uncertain how to properly dress for a job interview? Are you unclear what type of nonverbal messages you convey during the first few minutes of a job interview? Are you less concerned about your dress and appearance than in what you will say during a job interview?

IF YES: Before you even open your mouth to speak, your appearance has already made an impression. The old adage that *"You never get a second chance to make a first impression"* is especially relevant to the job interview. After all, you are meeting a stranger who knows little or nothing about you beyond your resume and perhaps a Google search. That stranger looks for clues as to why he or she should or should not hire you. Your nonverbal behavior, especially your dress and grooming, gives them important hiring indicators. If you dress and groom inappropriately for a job interview – wrong outfit, colors, accessories, jewelry, perfume, makeup, body piercing and art – you may be immediately knocked out of further consideration, regardless of what you say during the job interview. Your immediate dress and appearance will convey negative messages that will be difficult to overcome during the rest of the interview. Neglect your dress and appearance and you will quickly sabotage the job interview.

TIPS: Make the first few seconds of the interview work in your favor by nonverbally communicating your class, professionalism, and competence. Always dress appropriately for the occasion, which will vary depending on the type of job and organization. If you are interviewing for a professional position and most employees are expected to wear business attire, put on your best suit for the interview. If you are interviewing with a company where causal attire is the norm, try to dress one step above the norm. If you are interviewing for a blue collar position where a suit or sport coat would be inappropriate, be sure to dress conservatively and neatly. You don't want your attire to be a distraction – you either over-dressed or under-dressed for the occasion or you simply don't know how to put yourself together with appropriate colors, fabrics, styles, and quality. For useful tips on dress and image, see JoAnna Nicholson's *Dressing Smart for Women* and *Dressing Smart for Men*, and Susan Bixler's *The New Professional Image*. Young people may want to examine Joe Swinger's *Leave Your Nose Ring At Home*.

TIP #25
Prepare a list of questions you need to ask.

QUESTIONS: Do you need to prepare a set of questions to ask at the job interview? Are you uncertain which questions may have the greatest impact on your candidacy?

IF YES: Employers often report they are especially impressed with candidates who ask questions during interviews. When you ask questions, you indicate interest in the position as well as communicate your professionalism. Be prepared to ask several questions relevant to the job, employer, and organization. These questions should be designed to elicit information to help you make a decision as well as demonstrate your interest, intelligence, and enthusiasm for the job.

TIPS: You may want to write out several of these questions on a 3x5 card to help you remember the questions you want to ask. It's okay to refer to the card during the interview. Just mention to the interviewer that *"I have a few questions I wanted to ask you. I made some notes so I would be sure to ask them."* Then take out your notes and ask the questions. This indicates to the interviewer that you are prepared and have specific concerns he or she must also address. Questions you might want to ask about the company would revolve around areas not likely covered in materials you could have read before your interview. You want to know something about the following:

- Stability of the position and firm.
- Opportunities available for advancement.
- Management and decision-making styles – teams, hierarchies, degree of decentralization.
- Degree of autonomy permitted and entrepreneurship encouraged.
- Organizational culture.
- Internal politics.

Your questions may cover some of the following areas of inquiry:

- Why is this position open? Is it a new position? If not, why did the previous person leave? If the person was promoted, what position does that person now hold?

- How important is this position to the organization?

- To what extent does the company promote from within versus hiring from the outside?

- What plans for expansion (or cutbacks) are in the immediate future? What effect will these plans have on the position or the department in which it is located?

- How long do most employees stay with this company?

- Tell me about what it's really like working here in terms of the people, management practices, workloads, expected performance, and rewards.

- How would you evaluate the financial soundness and growth potential of this company?

- If you had to briefly describe this organization, what would you say? What about its employees? Its managers and supervisors? Its performance evaluation system? Its promotion practices?

- Assuming my work is excellent, where might you see me in another five years within this organization?

Questions about the job will relate more specifically to the day-to-day activities you could expect if you were to join this organization. You may wish to ask about some of the following concerns:

- How did this opening occur? Is it a newly created position or did someone recently leave the position?

- Tell me about the nature of the work I would be doing most of the time.

- What kinds of peripheral tasks would likely take up the balance of my time?

- What would be my most important duties? Responsibilities?

- What types of projects would I be involved with?

- What kinds of clients would I be working with?

- What changes is management interested in having take place within the direction of this department?

- What is the management style of the person who would be my supervisor?

- In what ways is management looking for this function [the function performed by the department I would be working in] to be improved?

- What have been the major problems [barriers to achieving department goals] in the past?

- What will be the major challenges for the person who is hired?

- How often would I be expected to travel?

You also should ask questions about the work environment. Consider asking some of these potentially revealing questions:

- Can you tell me something about the people I would be working with? Working for?

- How is performance evaluated? How often are such evaluation conducts? Who conducts the evaluations? What criteria are used in the evaluations? Does the employee have input into the evaluation? Do you have an annual performance appraisal system in place? How long has it been operating? How does it relate to promotions and salary increments? How do employees feel about this system?

- Can you tell me something about the company's management system? How do supervisors see their role in this company? Tell me about the person who would be my immediate supervisor.

- Is there much internal politics that would affect my position? Will I be expected to become part of anyone's group? How controversial is this hiring decision? Who is considered the most influential person in my division?

- Does the company provide in-house training? Does it support employees taking advantage of outside training in areas where it does not provide training programs? Is there support for employees returning to school for additional formal education?

- How open are opportunities for advancement? Assuming high performance, to what other positions might I progress?

TIP #26
Lessen your nervousness by following a few simple stress reduction techniques.

QUESTIONS: Do you often get nervous when speaking with strangers who have something important you want? Do you find job interviews to be stressful experiences? Would you like to reduce your stress and thus convey more confidence during job interviews?

IF YES: Job interviews are very stressful situations. Indeed, most job seekers approach the interview with sweaty palms and dry mouths. This is a time of great stress and nervousness. If you don't manage your stress and nervousness, you may have difficulty acing the interview.

TIPS: You can better control your nervousness by following the same advice often given to public speakers. As you walk into the interview room, try to take slow deep breaths. You can do this subtly so the interviewer will be unaware of it. And, although this is easier said than done, the more you can get your mind off yourself and concentrate on the other person, the more comfortable you will feel. If you are nervous, you are probably focusing too much attention on yourself. You are self-consciously concerned with how you are doing and what impression you are making on others. Try to be more other-directed. Rather than concentrate on your needs and fears, concern yourself with the employer's needs and questions.

Preparation is probably the greatest aid in lessening nervousness. If you prepared to both answer and ask questions and arrived on time, you should walk into the interview feeling well prepared and confident. If you arrive early for the interview, you will have a chance to collect your thoughts, take those deep breaths, and focus your attention toward the employer.

TIP #27
Expect to encounter multiple interviews
with a single employer.

QUESTIONS: Are you preparing for only one interview? Do you expect an employer to hire you after meeting you one or two times?

IF YES: Many interviewees are surprised to learn they are subjected to more than one interview with the same employer. Indeed, some candidates report being interviewed eight times with the same employer before being offered the job.

Most candidates normally experience two types of interviews: screening and hiring/placement. The screening interview may take place over the telephone. You must be prepared for that unexpected telephone call in which the employer probes your interest in the position, your availability, and your job-related expectations, including, perhaps, salary requirements. The hiring/placement interview is normally conducted in the interviewer's office. But it may involve a one-to-one interview or sequential, series, panel, or group interviews. This process could take place over a one- or two-week period in which you are called back to meet with other individuals in one-to-one, series, panel, or group interview situations. Each interview may probe a different level of your interests, abilities, knowledge, and skills.

TIPS: Be prepared to be invited to several interviews with the same employer. While it may be difficult to maintain a high level of energy and enthusiasm after the third or fourth interview, you do this by being well prepared and focused for each interview – treat that fourth interview the same way you would the first interview. After all, multiple interviews are tests of your ability to be consistent and persevere. At each interview, be prepared to talk about your accomplishments and ask thoughtful questions.

6

Actions Speak Louder Than Words
Making Good First Impressions

THE INTERVIEW IS ALL ABOUT making good first impressions both verbally and nonverbally. After all, you are meeting a group of strangers who need to make an important decision about your future and theirs – whether to hire you. While you made an initial good impression with your resume or application in order to get the job interview, now it's time to move from written impressions to making good face-to-face impressions.

In this chapter we reveal several tips to help you make that all important good first impression, even before you open your mouth. It's during those first five minutes – when you exchange greetings, shake hands, sit down, and engage in small talk – that important impressions are made which will largely determine whether or not you will be invited to another interview and eventually offered the job; the interviewer will already be making up of his or her mind about your candidacy. Do you look like you fit into the organization – from how you dress to how you handle small talk? Are you likable? Are you socially competent? Are you in the same socioeconomic class? Since you are literally being "sized up" at this time, it's extremely important that you manage those first impressions to your advantage.

TIP #28
Avoid alcohol and get a good night's sleep.

Since you need to communicate energy and enthusiasm throughout the job interview, make sure you get sufficient rest the night before the interview. Avoid alcohol or other stimulants or depressants that might interfere with your mental alertness and coherency. If you appear tired or run down, you will communicate very negative nonverbal messages about your ability to do the job.

TIP #29
Avoid tobacco products.

If you are a smoker, avoid smoking before the interview and make sure your clothes do not smell of smoke. Many employers will disqualify you if you are a smoker. After all, it's a bad personal habit that can negatively impact on the employer's health care costs. It may also result in absenteeism due to self-inflicted health problems. In addition, many people simply dislike being aro und smokers. All things being equal, most employers will hire a nonsmoker before they hire a smoker.

TIP #30
Organize your wardrobe and logistics.

It's a good idea to organize your wardrobe the day before the interview. Make sure your outfit is well coordinated and you are prepared to be well groomed from head to toe. Waiting until the last minute to pull together your interview clothes, shoes, and accessories is not smart preparation, especially when you discover that your best suit, blouse, or shoes are soiled or in disrepair.

TIP #31
Attend to personal hygiene before
you leave home.

Body oder and bad breath can quickly kill a job interview. Indeed, one of the first things interviewers notice is your scent. You need to look neat, clean, and well groomed throughout the job interview. That means attending to basic personal hygiene – bathing, brushing teeth, using mouthwash and deodorant, cleaning and clipping your fingernails, polishing your shoes, combing your hair, and wearing clean and well pressed clothes. Avoid excessive use of perfume, cologne, and aftershave which can be overpowering and thus leave a negative impression.

TIP #32
Call ahead to confirm the meeting time and place.

When you're invited to a job interview, it's incumbent upon you to make sure you know the exact interview time and place. Always ask for directions, even though you may have a good idea of where to go. Be realistic in estimating the amount of time it will take you to get to the street location as well as how long it will take to walk from the street to the office. Don't assume you will know how to get to the interview site just because you use Mapquest or your car is wired with a fancy navigation system. Too often this technology fails on the day of the interview and thus you may need to make embarrassing excuses for your lack of travel planning. Indeed, you may need some special directions, especially if the interview site is within a large office or industrial complex.

Showing up on time is extremely important to any job interview. If you fail to arrive on time, you will fail one of the most important steps in the job interview!

TIP #33
Call at least 24 hours ahead to cancel and/or reschedule an interview.

Certain circumstances may require you to cancel an interview: you become ill, a family emergency, a special work deadline, or another more promising interview. Be sure to call and explain your situation in as positive a manner as possible. Be very careful

Many people talk too much in the name of being honest and forthcoming.

what you say in this situation. Many individuals have a tendency to talk too much in the name of being honest and forthcoming. You don't need to tell the whole truth, which could raise a red flag, such as the fact that you scheduled an interview with a more attractive company, or your child is ill and you have to stay home with her. Just tell the person that you are unable to come to the interview at the designated time and ask if you could re-schedule the meeting at some mutually convenient time. That's all you need to say – nothing more. Spare the details. The conversation might go like this:

> *Hi, this is Lynn Baker. Tomorrow I'm scheduled for a 10 o'clock interview with Mr. Taylor. Unfortunately, I'm unable to meet at that time. Would it be possible to reschedule the interview for some time this Thursday or Friday?*

It's much better to speak in general terms than to confess the reasons behind your inability to make this appointment. Contrast the above neutral statement with these confessionals:

> *Hi, this is Lynn Baker. Tomorrow I'm scheduled for a 10 o'clock interview with Mr. Taylor. I'm unable to make it because ...*

- *I'm not feeling well – it's probably the flu.*
- *My daughter fell at school. I need to stay home with her tomorrow since I can't find anyone to take care of her.*
- *My car broke down.*
- *I can't get a ride – my driver's license is suspended.*
- *I have another interview scheduled at that time tomorrow.*
- *I was just assigned a new account which I have to meet about tomorrow.*
- *I have to take my mother to the doctor tomorrow.*

Such responses raise possible red flags that you may have health, child care, family, and responsibility issues that go beyond this interview situation. Is this an indicator of more scheduling and responsibility problems to come once you are hired? How often will you need to take off work and/or how frequently will you come to work late?

TIP #34
Plan to come alone.

Only **you** are invited to a job interview – not your parents, spouse, friend, or child. What kind of impression do you think you make when you greet the interviewer and then introduce your mother or spouse who accompanies you? If you bring a child with you because you couldn't find a baby-sitter, what message do you communicate to a potential employer about your childcare situation?

Arriving at an interview accompanied by someone else makes a very bad initial impression – you're not independent, you lack responsibility, and you're less than serious about the job. If someone does come with you to the interview site, make sure that person is not seen by anyone associated with the interview. Tell your relative or friend that you will call or meet at a specific place when you finish the interview. Your support system should be left at home, in the car, or outside rather than brought into the interview setting.

TIP #35
Arrive early.

While this may seem very elementary, you would be surprised how many candidates arrive late to job interviews – 10, 20, 30, or 40 minutes late! Most of them under-estimate the time it will take to get to the interview site, because they failed to plan their route, overlooked important details, such as finding parking and passing through security, or encountered unexpected delays along the way.

There's nothing worse than to arrive late for a job interview. Since the first five minutes of the interview are the most important, if you arrive five minutes late, you may effectively kill much of the interview – and your chances of getting the job. Your tardiness will be remembered and in a negative light.

Try to arrive at least ten minutes early. If need be, drive to the interview site the day before to estimate how long it will take you to get there as well as find parking. Allow plenty of time, anticipating that you could well lose a half hour or more to heavy traffic. In fact, add at least 30 minutes to your estimated travel time since you will probably need the extra time. When you arrive early, you'll have time to visit the restroom, talk to a few people, and survey your surroundings. You may notice some important clues about the company and people you will be meeting, such as an annual report, photos, or awards, which may raise some important questions you can ask, and help you with the initial small talk as you ease into the job interview.

TIP #36
Call if you may be late.

If you do encounter an unexpected delay that will put you late at the interview, be sure to call at least 10 minutes before the interview to let the interviewer know that you have encountered difficulties en route. If you don't, the interviewer will be left waiting, wondering, and wishing for another candidate. He or she may draw negative conclusions about your candidacy while watching his or her watch – *"This candidate can't even make it to the interview on time. I wonder what else I'll learn about him, if he comes at all?"* Your call indicates that you are a considerate individual who values the interview as well as the interviewer's time.

When you do call, just state the fact that it looks like you will be a little late. If your tardiness is due to an unexpected traffic delay, such as an accident, road closure, or bad weather (many individuals do have interviews scheduled during snowstorms and torrential rains!), briefly mention that fact when you call. If you will be late because of your lack of planning or a personal situation – got lost, overslept, or took care of a personal matter – don't admit what may be interpreted by the interviewer as a potential weakness (you have difficulty being on time for appointments) or the lack of responsibility. Just state the fact that it looks like you will be running 10 or 20 minutes late. When you do arrive late, apologize for being late – *"I'm really sorry to be late"* – and leave it at that. This is an embarrassing first encounter – hopefully forgettable – which you want to quickly put behind you.

TIP #37
Announce your presence.

Once you arrive at the interview site, announce who you are and the nature of your visit. Assuming you will initially walk into a reception area, walk up to the receptionist and simply state your name and the purpose of your visit, such as the following:

> *Hi, I'm Emily Harrison. I'm here for a one o'clock interview with Mr. Wilson.*

Don't address yourself as Mr. or Mrs., nor walk into another area unless invited to do so. Find a nearby seat and wait to be called for the meeting.

TIP #38
Visit the restroom.

If you arrive 10 to 15 minutes early, find a restroom to check on your grooming and take care of any personal matters. Is your hair in place? Do you need to reapply any makeup? Are your clothes, especially a necktie or scarf, aligned properly? Do you need to use the toilet? If the restroom is busy with employees, quickly get in and out without appearing too preoccupied with improving your appearance or engaging in small talk with strangers who might be important to a hiring decision. Indeed, you might unexpectedly meet the person who will soon interview you!

TIP #39
Drink some water.

Since job interviews can be stressful situations for many people – sweaty palms, dry throats, and cracking voice – drink some water just before you meet the interviewer. Better still, avoid eating salty foods the day prior to the interview – they may exacerbate an already stress-induced dry mouth. You don't want to be in the middle of an interview and discover your mouth is dry and you have trouble talking and hearing. Avoid taking any medications that might make you drowsy, incoherent, or inattentive.

TIP #40
Check your breath.

Even though you brushed your teeth and used mouthwash before leaving home, you still need to check and safeguard your breath before meeting the interviewer. To be on the safe side, assume that you may have a breath problem and thus use a mouth deodorant or breath mint just before entering the building.

TIP #41
Begin mentally preparing yourself for each
phase of the interview.

This should be your quiet time to think about certain things you want to say and do – mental cues to make sure you are making a good first impression. Rehearse in your mind the first five minutes of the interview –

.. you will greet the interviewer when you first meet, from standing up to a firm handshake and good eye contact; and the small talk you could initiate or a humorous story you might tell related to the interview or job. Then walk through each step of the interview. Restate your strategy for answering questions, especially behavioral questions; how you will handle questions related to possible red flags, salary, and objections to your candidacy. Recall three good examples of your accomplishments that you want to share with the interviewer; the questions you need to ask about the job, company, and current em-

Arrive in plenty of time so you can collect your thoughts and begin focusing on all phases of the interview.

ployees; how you plan to ask for the job as well as close the interview; and your plan to follow up the interview.

It's important that you arrive in plenty of time to refocus your mind on the important task ahead. If you are running late, you'll probably arrive at the interview stressed out from trying to get there on time. And you will probably carry that stress throughout the interview.

TIP #42
Be careful what you do and say in the reception area.

While you may think you are having a private moment waiting to be called in for the interview, chances are you are being observed and evaluated by others. What you say to others, such as a receptionist, and what you do while sitting, such as reading a magazine or playing with your phone, Blackberry, or iPod, may be reported to the interviewer after you leave. The interviewer may ask the receptionist what she thought of the candidate. If he learns that you were very rude, confused, or nervous, this report may negatively affect the outcome of your interview. If he learns that you were reading *People* magazine rather than the company's annual report, which also was on the table, you may seem superficial rather than serious about the job. Avoid using electronic devices while waiting – they may distract your mind from focusing on the interview, and they may reveal something about your interest in the job. This is the time when you should be doing your final mental preparation for the job interview. It's also a time when you can learn something about the company by observing your surroundings as well as asking a few questions of people you meet in the reception area.

TIP #43
Look like you've come for serious business.

Serious candidates project a professional image to everyone around them. They dress and groom properly, they ask employer-centered questions, they observe proper etiquette and social graces, and they appear to be nice people. They are initially "sized up" as being both likable and competent. Less serious candidates lack focus, arrive unprepared, talk too much about unrelated matters, use their time unwisely, and have attitude issues.

TIP #44
Manage your outerwear and accessories.

If you arrive at the interview wearing a coat and carrying an umbrella, take off your coat and leave it, along with the umbrella, in the reception area rather than drag these items into the interview room. If you take these items into the interview room, put them to the side, preferably on another chair. If you wear or hold your coat during the interview, you may appear anxious to leave or seem to be clinging to a security blanket! The only other things you should be carrying with you is a handbag (keep it small) or briefcase (also keep it small). Do not bring to the interview site any food, shopping bags, or other items unrelated to the interview.

TIP #45
Turn off your cell phone before you arrive at the interview site.

This tip relates to one of those "stupid mistakes job seekers make" that can greatly diminish your candidacy. While this may seem obvious, **phone etiquette** does become an issue in many job interviews these days. Indeed, there's nothing more embarrassing than to have your cell phone go off in the reception area or during the actual job interview! How do you recover from this self-inflicted error? You don't. If you fail to turn off your phone and it rings during the interview, immediately cut it off and apologize for the interruption. Show humility and some self-effacing humor to get through this moment: _"I'm so sorry about that. There's nothing more important to me than this interview, and I've just blew it!"_ You will be forgiven. Under no circumstances should you take the call!

TIP #46
Treat everyone you meet as important to the interview.

Interviewers sometimes ask their employees for reactions to candidates: *"What did you think about the candidate? Did you have a chance to talk to her? What did she do while she was waiting to meet me? Do you think you'll like working with her? Do you have any particular concerns?"* Employees' opinions can be very important to the interview process. So **make sure you treat everyone you meet as important to the interview**, regardless of where you meet them or their position. You'll never know who is the most trusted and influential employee until you've had a chance to work in the company.

TIP #47
Greet the interviewer properly.

Chances are the interviewer will come out to the reception area to greet you. Stand up straight, shake hands firmly, maintain eye contact, listen carefully, look energetic, speak in the positive, and introduce yourself: *"Hello, I'm Jane Morris. It's a pleasure to meet you."* Watch the small talk carefully. This is not a time to tell dumb jokes, look tired, appear nervous, or say something inane. If you are asked if you had any trouble finding the place or parking, appear competent and positive by indicating you handled this part of the interview with ease. If you've been so unfortunate as to arrive late for the interview, under no circumstances should you say something stupid like *"Sorry I'm late. I had difficulty finding this place since your directions were not very clear."* Say this and you'll be dead upon arrival!

TIP #48
Maintain good eye contact.

Eye contact is very important throughout the job interview. It establishes **rapport** with the interviewer. You appear interested in what is being said, and you will be perceived as more trustworthy if you look at the interviewer as you ask and answer questions. To say someone has "shifty eyes" or cannot "look us in the eye" is to imply they may not be completely honest. To have a direct, though moderate, eye gaze in our culture conveys interest as well as trustworthiness. Avoid excessive eye contact, which may make the interviewer uncomfortable.

TIP #49
Wait to be seated.

The particular seating arrangement for the interview may be important to the interviewer. You may, for example, be asked to sit on the other side of a desk or table. Alternatively, you may be invited to sit on a sofa. Whatever the case, don't look like you are in a hurry by taking a seat before you are invited to sit. Chances are you will be seated within six feet of the interviewer – a comfortable conversational distance for maintaining good eye contact.

TIP #50
Keep your feet on the floor.

If you are sitting on a sofa where your full body is in view, avoid crossing your legs and showing the soles of your shoes. Keep both feet on the floor. Crossed legs still indicate a degree of informality and familiarity that is unwarranted at this point in your relationship with the interviewer.

TIP #51
Appear to be a good listener by sitting forward
with a slight lean toward the interviewer.

How you sit and appear attentive can have positive outcomes in your job interview. For example, avoid leaning back in your chair or on the sofa looking extremely comfortable and relaxed. Such posture may communicate that you are more interested in talking about yourself than in listening to and learning from the interviewer. The best sitting posture is to sit erect and lean slightly forward toward the interviewer folding or steepling your hands. Nonverbally this communicates that you are interested in the interviewer. You will look more alert and energetic in this posture than in other positions.

TIP #52
Watch what you do with your hands, arms, and elbows.

If you are sitting at a desk, keep your hands, arms, and elbows off the desk and away from any distracting items such as pencils or pens. Try to look alert, energetic, and focused on the interviewer rather than fidget with items that indicate your nervousness or irritating habits. If you don't know what to do with your hands, try folding or steepling them. Keep them away from your mouth.

TIP #53
Carefully observe your surroundings for nonverbal cues.

If the interview takes place in an office, take a quick visual tour of everything around you – from the space, furniture, and artwork to photos, awards, and the view from the window. You may, for example, discover that the interviewer graduated from your college, she received a special award from a professional association, the company was featured in an important business magazine, or the African artwork represents a personal collection. If the office you're in has a big window overlooking the city, you might note its spectacular location.

The surroundings say something about the interviewer and the organization. Does this look like a quality company? Are the employees allowed to express their personalities in the way they organize their work space? Are there certain things here that would be good subjects for initiating small talk? Remember, the first five minutes of the interview, which may primarily focus on small talk, are the most important to the interview.

TIP #54
Let the interviewer initiate the openers, but take initiative when engaging in small talk.

It is the responsibility of the interviewer to initiate openers. During the first two or three minutes the interviewer will probably talk about your trip to the office, the weather, your impressions of the facilities, or some other small-talk topics. Respond to these questions with more than just *"yes"* or *"no"* answers and observations. You need to take some initiative here to express your personality. Initiate your own positive small talk by making an interesting observation about the office, such as the art work or decorating, or the personnel you met in the reception area. You might, for example, discover from seeing a framed degree hanging on the wall that the interviewer is a graduate of your alma mater. He or she may be a collector of unusual items that are displayed in the office. Or he or she may have an interesting photo displayed of family, friends, colleagues, a ceremony, or someone famous. Show some personal interest in the individual by focusing on one or two items for small talk. This small-talk period may result in building an important **personal bridge** between you and the interviewer that will make this professional encounter a much easier and more enjoyable one.

Remember, the most important impressions are made during the first five minutes. You want to appear energetic, positive, and interesting during these initial moments of the interview. In the end, how you handle yourself in the small-talk stage may be as important to getting the job as your responses to the standard interview questions.

TIP #55
Be prepared for typical opening questions.

At some point, probably within five minutes of meeting the interviewer, you will shift from small-talk to the substance of the interview – questions related to you and the job. Assuming you've handled yourself well at the greeting and small talk stage, now it's time to show your stuff – you're the right person for the job in question. At this point, the interviewer may give you some background information on the company and position and then ask you one of the following opening questions: *Tell me about yourself. Why are you interested in this position?* How you answer these questions may set the tone for the rest of the interview.

Let's examine the traditional first question:

Tell me about yourself.

This is a good question to get you talking about yourself and the job. Some interviewees mistakenly think that the interviewer wants them to give a verbal "resume" – summarize everything that's on the written resume. Others believe they are being asked to summarize their history – from when and where they were born to arriving for this job interview!

This question gives you an opportunity to literally "tell your story" – what it is you do well and enjoy doing and what you can do for the employer. Concentrate on communicating your **pattern of accomplishments** to the interviewer – the single most important piece of information interviewers need in the hiring process.

7

Anticipate Questions and Tell Your Story

THE HEART OF THE JOB INTERVIEW usually involves a one-on-one conversation with an interviewer. How you handle this conversation and the answers you give to specific questions will largely determine whether or not you will be invited to additional interviews and eventually offered the job.

The following tips should help you handle the job interview scenario. They primarily focus on questions you are likely to be asked and the type of answers that will most impress interviewers.

TIP #56
Outline what you want to achieve in the interview.

What exactly do you want to achieve in the job interview? Do you have specific goals? Or are you just planning to go with the flow – see what happens after you show up? We strongly recommend that you look at a job interview as an opportunity to achieve specific goals. If you do so, you will be able to better prepare for the interview as well as stay focused throughout the interview. For example, your goals might include the following:

1. Learn more about the position and your responsibilities.
2. Determine whether or not you would be happy working there.
3. Identify whom you would be working with – both supervisors and co-workers.
4. Uncover performance expectations and evaluation system.
5. Understand how you might advance within the company.
6. Discover what problems you would be expected to solve.
7. Communicate your accomplishments to the interviewer.
8. Get invited to another interview and offered the job.

If your only goal is to get a job offer, you may overlook many other important considerations, such as whether or not this job would be a good fit for your particular interests and skills. When you outline your goals, you will discover how important it is to engage in a dialogue rather than just prepare to answer anticipated questions with model answers supplied by so-called interview Q&A experts. Indeed, you may want to ask numerous questions about the position, company, and your future.

TIP #57
Leave your internal critic at home.

We all have an **internal coach** – that voice in your head that supports you, encourages you, and propels you forward as it says you **can** accomplish the task at hand. As the same time, you may have an internal critic – that voice of negativity that says you will not succeed. Your internal critic asks, *"How am I doing?"* as you engage in the interview or, even worse, keeps up a barrage of negatives: *"I am doing terribly; I must really sound stupid; this interview isn't going well; I am never going to get this job offer."* The constant negatives may keep you from being your best "in the moment." These negatives also create a self-fulfilling prophecy of making you nervous!

Leave your internal critic at home. On the way to your interview, concentrate on your **strengths** as they relate to the job, and as you greet the interviewer and engage in dialogue, let your energy work in positive ways to convey your enthusiasm and dynamism in dialogue with the interviewer.

It will help if you keep the focus off yourself and how you are doing. Focus on the interviewer and the exchange of information. Remember, this may not be "the" job for you. Concentrate on selling your strengths (another job opening now or in the future may be "the right one") and finding o ut abo ut the position and the o rganization. Fo rget abo ut yourself, and focus instead on the employer, the organization, and the problems the employer needs solved.

TIP #58
Take notes.

If one of your goals is to acquire more information about the job and organization, you are well advised to take notes during the interview. Take a pad of paper with you to the interview and write down important information you acquire during your conversations. As you learn more about the job and company, you may wish to jot down questions that you will want to address later in the interview. You'll find your notes will come in handy at the end of the interview; at that time you will want to close by summarizing your understanding of the position. In addition, when you take notes, you impress upon the interviewer that you are a serious candidate who is taking down important information as part of your decision-making process.

TIP #59
Prepare for traditional interview questions.

You should be prepared to address several different types of questions during the job interview. Assuming you know yourself and have done all the necessary research for anticipating the interview situation, you next need to prepare for both general and specific interview questions. Although you cannot anticipate in advance the exact questions the interviewer will ask, you can anticipate the general lines of inquiry. You can expect to be asked questions regarding your education, your work experience, your career goals, and how you get along with others. Many questions will be historical in nature, probing your background. For management positions, questions about your management style, management philosophy, as well as questions about specific experiences you have encountered and how you handled them are likely to be asked. Some of the following questions will certainly arise during the interview:

Your Education

- Describe your educational background.
- Why did you attend _____ University (or College)?
- Why did you major in _____ ?
- What was your grade point average?
- What subjects did you enjoy the most? The least? Why?
- What leadership positions did you hold?
- How did you finance your education?
- If you were to start over, what would you change about your education?
- Why were your grades so low? So high?
- Did you do the best you could in school? If not, why not?

Your Work Experience

- What were your major achievements in each of your past jobs?
- Why did you change jobs before?
- What is your typical workday like?
- What functions do you enjoy doing the most?
- What did you like about your boss? Dislike?
- Which job did you enjoy the most? Why? Which job did you enjoy the least? Why?
- Have you ever been fired? Why?

Your Career Goals

- Why do you want to join our organization?
- Why do you think you are qualified for this position?
- Why are you looking for another job?
- Why do you want to make a career change?
- What ideally would you like to do?
- Why should we hire you?
- How would you improve our operations?
- What is the lowest pay you will take?
- How much do you think you are worth for this job?
- What do you want to be doing five years from now?
- How much do you want to be making five years from now?
- What are your short-range and long-range career goals?

- If you could choose your company, where would you go?
- What other types of jobs are you considering? Other companies?
- When will you be ready to begin work?
- How do you feel about relocating, traveling, working overtime, and spending weekends in the office?
- What attracted you to our company?

Your Personality and Other Concerns

- Tell me about yourself.
- What are your major weaknesses? Your major strengths?
- What causes you to lose your temper?
- What do you do in your spare time? Any hobbies?
- What types of books do you read?
- What role does your family play in your career?
- How well do you work under pressure? In meeting deadlines?
- Tell me about your management philosophy.
- How much initiative do you take?
- What types of people do you prefer working with?
- How _____ (creative, analytical, tactful, etc.) are you?
- If you could change your life, what would you do differently?
- Who are your references?

We list several additional questions you may be asked in the Appendix at the end of this book.

TIP #60
Be prepared to handle red flag questions.

In addition to these general areas of inquiry, ask yourself what other questions the interviewer might ask given your particular background, resume, and references. For example:

- Do you have any time gaps that are unaccounted for in your work or educational history?

- Have you held numerous jobs or attended several schools in a relatively short time span?

- Does your work history show a pattern of lateral or downward movement within or between organizations?

- Are you applying for a job with less responsibility/pay than your present or most recent job?

- Do you have a criminal record that is likely to be uncovered through a background check or may appear on your resume or application as a major employment gap?

Employers look for red flags on resumes and applications and when you answer and ask questions during interviews. Not surprisingly, when employers find serious red flags, they will not hire you unless something extraordinary happens to change their mind, such as the fact that you have a hard-to-find skill or you have strong positive recommendations.

While you should not volunteer information about red flags in your background, you should be prepared to answer such questions that might come up any time during a job interview. For example, the interviewer might look at your resume and raise the following red flag questions:

- *I noticed you attended XYZ college for two years but never graduated. Why didn't you complete a degree?*

- *I see you've held four different jobs during the past five years. Why did you change jobs so often?*

- *You have very little work experience. Why should we hire you?*

They may also ask you the following sensitive questions:

- *Have you ever been fired?*

- *Have you ever been convicted of a crime?*

You need to develop a **strategy** as to how you will address such questions. Acknowledge the facts about your background but go on to turn what initially appears to be a negative into a positive. If, for example, you appear to be a job hopper, because you have a history of frequent job changes, the interviewer will most likely ask you this potential knock-out question:

> *I see from your application that you've worked for four employers during the past five years. That concerns me since our average employee has been with us for 3½ years. Why did you change jobs so often?*

This question might be followed up with another obvious question:

> *If we offer you this job, how long do you expect to stay with our company?*

> *What do you see as being different here that would cause you to stay three to five years?*

Think carefully before you answer these questions. What were your previous situations? Were you fired, your company downsized, you lost interest, advanced your career, took short-term or temporary jobs for financial reasons, or worked in a high turnover industry? Whatever your situation or reasons, try to put the best face on it you honestly can and take responsibility. Here's a possible positive response to the initial job hopping question:

> *I know four employers in five years may raise a red flag about my willingness to stay with an employer. But let me explain what happened. My first two jobs as a waiter had nothing to do with my career interests or long-term plans. They were really temporary jobs that helped me financially get through a two-year certification program in telecommunications. Upon completing the program, I landed a job with a telecommunications firm. Unfortunately, and to everyone's surprise, that company went out of business within six months. I then moved to another telecommunications firm which also went out of business within a year. I had no idea how volatile the telecommunications field was when I started school. In fact, this was one of the hottest fields around a few years ago and then the bubble burst right at the time I started my new career. I'm looking for a stable employer, such as you, who plans to be in*

business for a long time and who values your employees. That's what attracted me to your company. I've heard many good things about it being one of the best companies to work for in this region. I would expect to stay with you as long as possible. I see this as a place where I can grow professionally in a long and productive career working with a very exciting group of people. Given my last two jobs with companies that closed, I do have a few questions about this company and its future.

There are many other possible scenarios relating to job-hopping concerns. If you indeed are a serial job hopper who has difficulty staying with an employer for a reasonable period of time, you'll need to convince this employer that you are now different; your pattern of behavior has changed. Give examples of what you have done, as well as what you intend to do, that will make a difference. But if you look like a job hopper because you were fired from your last four jobs, you are well advised to seek professional help in dealing with what may well be some serious personal- and work-related issues.

We address these and many other red flag questions in a separate interview book, *Job Interview Tips for People With Not-So-Hot Backgrounds: How to Put Red Flags Behind You to Win the Job*.

TIP #61
Anticipate behavior-based questions.

Don't be surprised to encounter behavior-based questions during job interviews. Indeed, more and more employers prefer asking behavior-based questions these days, because they know candidates cannot prepare answers to most such questions. They believe that how a job candidate has responded to certain types of situations in the past is a good predictor of how that person will behave in a similar future situation. Behavior-based questions are likely to begin with some variation of:

- *Give me an example of time when . . .*
- *Give me an example of how you . . .*
- *Tell me about how you . . .*
- *Describe a situation in which you . . .*

These questions are usually followed up with more probing questions, such as:

- *What did you specifically do in that situation?*
- *Why did you decide to take that course of action?*
- *If you had to do it over again, what might you do differently?*
- *How has that experience influenced your approach to . . . ?*

This is an opportunity for you to sell your positives with an example or two. Briefly describe the situation, enthusiastically explain what you did (adding information as to why, if you think this would not be evident), and indicate the outcome. Try to draw lessons that might apply to the job for which you are interviewing. Remember, the interviewer asks these types of questions because he is looking for **predictable patterns of behavior** that can be applied to his company.

For example, if the interviewer asks,

Tell me about a time when you saved a company account.

The applicant might respond,

Just last month I was observing a one-day training session conducted by one of our instructors I supervise. His class evaluations were lower than what we expect of our trainers, and my boss told me the client was not happy with the way the training sessions were going. He was afraid we might lose the account.

As I observed the session it was apparent the instructor knew the material but was having trouble moving the participants through the material in the time allotted. They often broke into small groups to complete an activity, but it was taking a long time, as some groups had to wait for others to finish. At the end of the day Joe and I met with the client who indicated his dissatisfaction and gave us an ultimatum: if the training of future groups couldn't be completed in a day and to his satisfaction, he would get another contractor.

I solved the problem by having Joe develop copies of the end product the participants should have formulated at the end of each segment of the activity. At the next training session he was able to pass these out at the end of the allotted time for each phase of the activity.

The seminar participants understood the information and gave the instructor excellent course evaluations and the client was pleased. We not only saved this contract, but got an additional contract from the client as well. My boss and I were both pleased with the outcome.

Obviously you want to select examples that promote your skills and have a positive outcome. Even if the interviewer asks about a time when something negative happened, try to select an example where you were able to turn the situation around and something positive came out of it. For example, if asked, *"Tell me about a time you made a bad decision,"* try to identify an example where:

- even though it wasn't the best decision, you were able to pull something positive out of the situation.

- though it was a poor decision, you learned from it and in the next similar situation you made a good decision, or you know how you will handle it differently the next time a similar situation arises.

- it was a bad decision but the negative outcome had only minimal impact.

In other words, try to pull something positive – either that you did or that you learned – out of even a negative experience you are asked to relate. The employer is interested in the process you went through and the reasoning behind your actions – not just the outcome. As you prepare for your interview, consider situations where you:

- demonstrated leadership
- solved a problem
- increased company profits
- made a good decision/made a poor decision
- handled change (not money, but changing events)
- handled criticism

- met a deadline/missed a deadline
- worked as part of a team

Add to this list other behavioral questions you think of that apply to the job for which you are interviewing. For example, if the job includes making presentations, expect questions about a speech where you achieved your goal or conversely about a time when your speech failed miserably.

Ask others who have interviewed with the company, if possible, what types of questions to expect. You may encounter hypothetical questions in which you are asked not what you did, but what you would do *if* something occurred. With hypothetical questions the interviewer is usually not interested so much in your actual answer – often there is no correct or incorrect response – as in your thought process. The information is in how you would solve a problem or respond to a particular type of situation.

Anticipate questions you might be asked so you can prepare a well thought-out response prior to the interview. Be ready to give examples and details of what you did (process) and what happened (outcome). You need to be able to back up your assertions with support. Go to the interview prepared with examples, statistics, and testimonials. When asked how you handled a situation, you have examples ready to relate. When you assert that your re-organization of a department resulted in improved customer service, you can back this up by indicating that customer complaints decreased by 55 percent after you instituted changes. When you say that you were a star salesperson, you can add that your company recognized you with the "First Place Sales Award" two years in a row. Be prepared to answer the interviewer's questions with a truthful, yet positive pitch and then support your pitch with examples, illustrations, statistics, or testimonials. It is far easier to formulate positive responses to questions in the relaxed setting of your living room than in the stressful and time-constrained setting of the job interview.

As we noted in Chapter 5, the following books, which are jam-packed with strategies and sample questions, will help you prepare for behavioral-based interviews:

High-Impact Interview Questions
Competency-Based Interviews
Preparing for the Behavior-Based Interview

TIP #62
Understand situational interviews.

More and more employers also are conducting situational interviews, which enable them to **observe the actual behavior** of candidates in particular situations. While candidates can prepare for behavioral interviews by focusing on their **accomplishments** and telling **stories** about their past **performance** that communicate a clear **pattern of behavior**, such interviews are still primarily verbal exchanges. Employers analyze answers to open-ended questions for clues of future performance.

Situational interviews rely less on analyzing verbal cues and more on analyzing both verbal and nonverbal behavior. Employers especially like conducting these interviews because they know candidates can't prepare well for the situations in which they may be asked to perform. These interviews give employers a chance to observe a candidate's decision-making skills in the process of solving work-related problems. Many of these interviews involve mock scenarios in which a candidate is asked to role play. For example, someone who is interviewing for a customer service position may be asked to play the role of a customer service representative by handling telephone calls from an irate customer. In this scenario the interviewer has a chance to observe how the candidate actually handles such a customer. Does he or she talk down to the customer, get angry, or resolve the problem to the satisfaction of the customer, who hopefully will become a repeat customer? The behavior of a competent customer service representative can be readily observed in such a role-playing scenario. Other examples of situational interviews may involve mock negotiation sessions, selling a product, counseling a client, teaching a course, constructing something, or repairing a product.

Employers like to conduct situational interviews because they know candidates can't prepare well for the situations in which they may be asked to perform.

You really can't do much to prepare for a situational interview since such interviews require you to demonstrate specific skills in reference to an employer's unstated performance criteria. Just know that you might be asked to perform. When faced with such a task-oriented situation, you need to approach it in a very calm and professional manner, however stressful the situation may be.

TIP #63
Anticipate brainteaser questions and puzzles.

Frequently used by Microsoft and other fast-paced high-tech, finance, and consulting companies, brainteaser questions and puzzles are basically designed to test your intelligence, resourcefulness, and enthusiasm for tackling problems. For example, you might be asked these questions, which do not have a correct or wrong answer:

If you had to eliminate one of the 50 states, which one would you take out and why?

Why are manhole covers round?

How many hair dryers are found in the hotels of New York City?

You have three buckets and 23 tennis balls. How can you get an even number of balls in each of the buckets?

Information technology firms, which frequently ask such questions, will ask more technically-oriented questions appropriate for the job.

Brainteaser questions and puzzles share one thing in common – for the interviewee, they are stressful. They may be asked any time during the interview. In fact, some interviewers like to start out an interview with a brainteaser question.

Interviewers ask these questions in order to see how bright you are, especially if you are capable of quickly thinking outside the box. In addition, such questions are used as indicators of a candidate's ability to be creative, curious, and logical. Answers to brainteaser questions require you to immediately think on your feet and come up with answers that impress the interviewer. If you're good at answering such questions, you'll demonstrate your mental agility in a stressful situation. If you hesitate and can't give good answers, you may be knocked out of consideration because you seem to lack creativity, initiative, and the ability to take charge of a situation. Worse, you may appear dim-witted, slow, or "not too bright."

In preparation for brainteaser questions, we recommend the following books that focus on this subject:

How Would You Move Mount Fuji
How to Ace the Brainteaser Interview
Programming Interviews Exposed

TIP #64
Beware of trick questions.

Some interviewers like to throw in trick questions in order to test a candidate's ability to handle stress and come up with clever answers. For example, you might be asked the following:

Sell this Blackberry to John, who does our janitorial work
on weekends. How will you approach him and what will you say
to convince him to buy something he ostensibly doesn't need?

In this case, the interviewer is not really expecting you to convince John that he needs this piece of technology. Instead, he wants to see how you've analyzed this situation and whether or not you've developed a clever strategy to sell someone something he doesn't obviously need. If you are an "I can sell anyone anything" type of person, you should be able to think up a very unique and creative strategy for impressing the interviewer. You might respond with a couple of clarification questions, such as _"Are you planning to promote John soon?"_ or _"When will John retire?"_ Then turn to your subject by focusing on the importance of communicating with members of John's family on weekends with what is now a very inexpensive but powerful device that will also enable John to track sports and view movies during his down time.

TIP #65
Keep your cool when faced with stress questions.

Interviewers often ask stressful questions in order to see how candidates best handle stress. Indeed, if a job involves a great deal of stress, the interviewer may throw out several hypothetical questions intended to elicit responses to stressful situations. For example, you may be asked how you would handle a client who threatens to sue the company because of your actions. What would you do as a supervisor if one of your employees has mental health issues that threaten fellow employees?

At the same time, you might be asked a very pointed question about your background and qualifications:

I'm really not comfortable with your so-called management experience at Container CSR. What did you accomplish there that especially qualifies you for this job?

If you've prepared well for the interview and can give examples of accomplishments relevant to the position, you should be able to answer this question with ease.

As a general rule, always remember that the job interview, by definition, is a stressful experience that you must go through in order to get the job offer. **Regardless of the questions asked, always keep your cool.** Listen carefully, answer calmly, use positive language, don't talk too much or too fast, and always appear both interested and enthusiastic even about the most negative questions thrown at you. In the end, you want to be **remembered** as someone who can handle the pressure of work and relationships.

TIP #66
Put yourself in the shoes of the interviewer.

Always put yourself in the shoes of the interviewer as you both prepare for the job interview and participate in the actual interview. Ask yourself, *"As an employer, what exactly do I want to know about and learn from this candidate?"* If you constantly ask yourself this question, you should become more employer-centered in how you both answer and ask questions. You'll focus on communicating your qualifications to the employer. You'll give examples of what you have accomplished in the past and ask questions about what you can do for the employer in the future. In other words, you'll tell a compelling story that will command the attention of the interviewer. If you fail to put yourself in the interviewer's shoes, chances are you may do what many other failed candidates do – focus on their own needs by asking self-centered questions, such as "What does the job pay? How many vacation days will I receive? Do you offer dental insurance? What about your pension plan? When can I start?" While these questions need to be asked, you should only focus on them **after** you have received a job offer and just before you either accept or reject that offer.

TIP #67
Listen carefully to the interviewer and appear open to his thoughts and ideas.

Most employers are not interested in hiring closed-minded individuals who don't listen and follow directives. After all, they expect you will have to learn about their operations. If you listen very carefully to what the interviewer says, you should pick up clues as to specific needs of the employer. You want to identify what problems the company faces as well as learn about possible solutions appropriate to the company. Be careful in offering solutions to problems you do not understand and a company you are unfamiliar with. Your proposed solutions may appear naive or, even worse, offend certain well established employees who are not particularly interested in hiring an outsider. Keep an open mind by asking questions about how the interviewer and others in the organization view the problem as well as the solution. Learn as much as possible about the internal operation of the organization, especially the key players with whom you will work and who will influence your work life. Ask some of these questions to gain knowledge about the interpersonal dynamics of the position:

- *Whom will I be working with?*
- *Can you tell me something about them and their work?*
- *How long have they been with the company?*
- *Of all the people I'll be working with, which ones do you consider to be your most reliable?*
- *Whom would you recommend I turn to for assistance?*
- *What do you see as the major problems related to my position?*
- *Will I be replacing someone or is this a new position?*
- *Can you tell me about the people who last held this position?*
- *How long did she stay?*
- *Why did she leave?*
- *Would it be okay if I talked to her about this position?*
- *What might she tell me, or not tell me?*
- *What issues did she face and how did she deal with them?*
- *Were you generally pleased with her work?*
- *Are there certain potholes here that I should be aware of?*
- *What do you see as your biggest challenges ahead?*

- *How does my position relate to those challenges?*
- *Can you tell me a little more about how you plan to solve these problems?*
- *What has been done so far?*
- *What other ideas have been considered?*

This line of questioning impresses upon the interviewer that you are an inquisitive person who listens and is open to others' ideas. You are interested in learning from others before drawing conclusions and making decisions. In other words, you have a non-threatening personality, one that might fit well with other personalities in the organization.

TIP #68
Don't interrupt or cut the interviewer off.

As you probably learned as a child, it's rude to interrupt other people who are talking. Unfortunately, many adults continue such behavior in both social and professional situations. While you may be anxious to talk because you have so much to contribute to a conversation, it's best to wait your turn in a job interview. If you have a tendency to jump into the middle of conversations, step back and start looking for cues as to when it's your turn to speak. If you listen carefully, you will pick up such cues.

Throughout the interview you should demonstrate good **listening skills**. When the interviewer is talking, you need to listen carefully and wait your turn to speak. If you miss your cues and interrupt, you will be seen as someone who doesn't listen, who is aggressive, and who is primarily concerned with listening to himself talk. No one wants to hire such self-centered individuals who probably won't listen on the job!

TIP #69
Be polite and show respect and tolerance.

Believe it or not, employers prefer hiring people they **like**. Indeed, **likability** ranks near the top of most employer's hiring criteria. And they especially like people who are polite, show respect, and are tolerant of others. In other words, you need to demonstrate good social graces from the moment you arrive at the interview to the time you close and leave the interview site.

TIP #70
Use positive form throughout the interview.

The way you phrase your questions and answers can be as important as the actual content of your communication. What you want to achieve is **positive form**. This means avoiding negatives by presenting yourself in as positive a light as possible. In the interview, several opportunities arise for enhancing your image through the use of positive form.

The first use of positive form relates to **names**. Each of us likes to be called by our name. Make sure you get the name of the interviewer, get it right, and use it from time to time as you speak. Use the interviewer's title (Miss, Mrs., Mr., Dr., Professor, etc.) and last name. **Never** call the interviewer by his or her first name unless specifically requested to do so – even if the interviewer uses your first name. Many interviewers will be offended by such familiarity.

A second use of positive form is inherent in the **way you phrase questions and answers**. For example, rather than ask *"What are the duties of_____ position?,"* ask *"What would be my duties?"* This form of questioning subtly plants the positive thought of you in the position. This is not presumptuous because you use the word *"would,"* which indicates you are not overly sure of yourself.

A third use of positive form relates to **good grammar**. Proper use of language is not something to be left in the English classroom. Many so-called "educated" people do not use good grammar, and many of these people do not interview successfully. Check your use of grammar. If it is not impeccable, make an effort to improve it before the interview.

Fourth, use **good diction**. One of the most common problems is to shorten words. How many people do you hear say *"goin'"* instead of *"going,"* or *"gonna"* rather then *"going to"*? Another problem is substituting, eliminating, or adding consonants: *"Adlanta"* rather than *"Atlanta,"* *"din't"* rather than *"didn't,"* *"idear"* rather than *"idea."* Do you do this? Do you ever say *"yea"* instead of *"yes"*? The use of sloppy speech is a habit many people – including the well educated – get into. But it is a habit – a learned and reinforced behavior – you can change. If you have a tendency to modify words in this manner, it is a habit worth correcting.

Fifth, avoid using **vocalized pauses**. An occasional silence is acceptable and preferable to overuse of *"ah's"* and *"uhm's."* Try not to fill silences with *"ah"* or *"and ah."* Vocalized pauses distract the listener from your message and the excessive use can be annoying.

Sixth, avoid the use of **fillers**. Fillers add no information and, if overdone, also distract the listener. The most commonly used fillers are *"you know,"* *"like,"* and *"okay."* If used frequently, the listener becomes distracted and will find it hard to concentrate on the content of your message.

Seventh, use **active verbs**. When talking about what you have done or will do, active verbs such as *"organized,"* *"analyzed,"* or *"supervised"* are preferable to the nouns *"organizer,"* *"analyst,"* or *"supervisor."* Avoid the passive voice. For example, instead of saying *"The entire conference was organized by me"* (passive vo ice), say *"I organized the entire conference"* (active voice).

Eighth, avoid using **tentative, indecisive terms**, such as *"I think,"* *"I guess,"* *"I feel."* If you use them excessively, they will negatively affect the impression you are trying to leave with the interviewer. Research indicates that women use these tentative terms more frequently than men. By using these indecisive terms, you can, regardless of your gender, appear indecisive and somewhat muddled. You want to communicate that you are a clear and purposeful individual.

Ninth, avoid the use of **ambiguous** and somewhat **negative terms** such as *"pretty good"* or *"fairly well."* These terms say little if anything. They may even communicate negatives – that what you did was not good!

Most people could improve their use of positive form. But it is difficult for someone to follow those suggestions after reading them the night before the interview. One needs to begin making the necessary changes well in advance of the interview. It can be done if one really wants to make the changes, but for most people it takes concerted effort over time. By all means, do not pass up these nine opportunities for using positive form in the interview.

TIP #71
Give examples and use supports.

Public speakers are always advised to analyze both their audience and their situation before speaking. The same advice should be followed when you interview. **The language you use should vary according to the interviewer.** If the interviewer is from the personnel office with little or no background in your field of expertise, your language should be less technical than it would be if you were talking with someone who shares your technical background. If you are interviewing with someone in your area of expertise, who also has the technical background, you should use a vocabulary relevant to the job in order to build common ground as well as your credibility. But don't overdo the use of jargon.

Analysis of your situation should tell you this is not the time for excessive modesty. Of course, you do not want to become an obnoxious braggart, but you do want to present your strengths – skills and accomplishments – in a positive way. Therefore, don't be reluctant to **talk about yourself and your accomplishments.** Remember, the interviewer wants to know more about you, especially your potential value to him or her. The more positive information you can communicate to the interviewer, the stronger your position will be in the final hiring decision.

When you make statements about your skills or accomplishments, try to back them up with **supports.** Can you give an **example** of how you improved production on your last job? Can you **describe** the sales campaign that won you the Best-Copywriter-of-the-Year Award? Can you **compare** the previous bookkeeping system with the one you instituted that saved your last employer so much money? Can you cite **figures** that demonstrate how you increased sales at the last company you worked for?

When you back up your assertions with supports, you gain several advantages over individuals who do not. Supports help clarify your comments, help substantiate them, help the listener recall them at a later time, and they add interest. Supports include such things as:

- examples
- illustrations
- descriptions
- statistics
- comparisons
- testimonials
- definitions

Use such supports to emphasize your accomplishments. If you choose to take a professional portfolio to the interview, it can be an excellent aid in demonstrating your accomplishments.

A frequent question asked by prospective interviewees is *"How honest should I be?"* Most individuals have something in their background they believe would work against them in getting the job if the interviewer knew about it. They wonder if they should tell the interviewer before he or she finds out. We advise you to be honest – but not stupid. In other words, if asked a direct question about the thing you hoped to hide, answer honestly, but emphasize positives. Under no circumstances should you volunteer your negatives or weaknesses. The following section will show you how to manage questions about your weaknesses.

TIP #72
Avoid short and incomplete answers.

The verbal interchange still remains extremely important in determining interview outcomes. Interviewers want to engage you in a conversation in order to learn more about you. Based on this conversation, they look for cues about your motivation, goals, choices, intelligence, and ability to work with others. They want to listen to what you say, analyze your thinking, and draw conclusions about your personality and behavior based upon this conversation. If you respond to every question with short answers, you indicate a lack of substance or depth. You also may appear to be anti-social or noncommunicative.

Be prepared to answer questions with substance. Part of your interview preparation should involve timing your answers to questions. This is not to suggest you memorize answers and time them. But time a few of your responses to get a feel for how long a 30-second to two-minute response is – what it feels like. Vary the length of your answers. For example, each question should elicit a 30-second to two-minute response from you. If your responses are less than 30 seconds, you may make the interviewer feel uneasy about the progress of the interview. Indeed, he may decide to shorten the interview and remove you from further consideration since you have little to tell him beyond what appears on your resume.

The same is true once you are outside the formal interview setting. If, for example, you are invited to lunch or dinner with a few employees, be sure to keep the conversation flowing with small talk related to your work and the company with which you are interviewing. If you are shy in such situations, especially engaging in conversation with strangers, you may want to develop some useful small-talk skills by reading a few of these books:

The Fine Art of Small Talk
How to Work a Room
How to Make People Like You in 90 Seconds or Less
How to Talk So People Listen
How to Start a Conversation and Make Friends
How to Talk to Anyone
The Art of Mingling
What Do I Say Next?

TIP #73
Don't talk too much.

The corollary to giving very short answers to interview questions and failing to engage in small talk is to talk excessively. Indeed, one of the worst interview sins you can commit is to talk too much. Some of the most memorable candidates, those who are usually rejected for positions, are those who talk too much – motor mouths! They seem more interested in listening to themselves talk than in listening to the interviewer and giving thoughtful yet succinct answers to questions. They also tend to volunteer unnecessary and damaging information about themselves and others. Candidates who are big talkers are usually viewed as potential problem employees. Once hired, they will probably irritate everyone around them by talking too much! You need to know when it's time to stop talking and begin listening to others around you.

TIP #74
Don't volunteer sensitive information.

Interviewees who talk too much often volunteer sensitive information that may raise red flags about their candidacy as well as make the interviewer feel uncomfortable. For example, it's not unusual for candidates to volunteer information about their personal lives which normally would be considered illegal questions (Tip #18) for employers to ask – religion, age, disability, marital status, health problems, mental health issues, number of children, child care situation, spouse's occupation, sexual orientation, financial status, housing issues, political preferences, and criminal record. The old saying that people say the dumbest things especially pertains to many individuals who interview for jobs!

TIP #75
Answer questions with complete sentences – and with substance.

Avoid simple *"yes"* or *"no"* answers. Remember, the interviewer is looking for **indicators of substance and benefits**. Brief answers give little information about you. They may indicate a lack of interest or substance on your part. The interviewer should leave this interview thinking *"I feel good about this person. He gave good answers to my questions."* If you don't answer the questions completely, how can the interviewer feel good about you?

TIP #76
Always emphasize the positive.

You want both the content of your responses and the manner in which you phrase your answers to be positive. As you talk about your previous employer(s), try to cast them in as positive a view as possible. After all, if you talk negatively about a former employer, the prospective employer will assume that someday you'll talk that way about him. If you bad-mouth your former company, the employer will expect that one day you'll do the same to his. If you have only negative remarks about your co-workers, he will question your ability to get along in his organization as well. In other words, you have little to gain – and much to lose – during the interview by venting frustrations about previous jobs.

Try to put on the most positive "spin" possible – honest, but not stupid – as you phrase thoughtful responses. Avoid negative words like *"can't," "didn't," "wouldn't,"* and phrase your answers with positive words instead. Rather than say, *"I wouldn't want to travel more than 4 or 5 days per month,"* you could respond with a more positive, *"I would prefer to keep my travel to 4 or 5 days per month."* Practice being more positive in your day-to-day communication and you will find it will come to you more easily in an interview.

TIP #77
Turn potential negatives into positives.

While interviewers also want to know what's wrong about you – your negatives – you want to continuously stress your positives – what's right about you. You can do this by maintaining a positive orientation toward all questions.

Most applicants, for example, have some qualification or lack of a qualification that they, as well as potential employers, may consider to be a negative that is likely to knock them out of consideration for the position. Perhaps you are just out of school and hence don't have experience. Maybe you are over 50 and, although you know it is illegal for an employer to discriminate against you on the basis of your age, you believe this will be a hindrance to your getting a job. Perhaps you have not stayed in your past jobs for very long and your resume shows a pattern of job hopping. Maybe your grades in school were average at best.

Whatever the negatives you believe will hinder your efforts at landing a job, you should attempt to find a way to turn the negative into an honest positive. Caryl recalls an older woman – well into her sixties – who came into her office where she was the personnel director several years ago. The woman evidently thought her age would be a negative, so she came prepared with several advantages to hiring someone her age. Her first advantage was that she *"would not get pregnant!"*

TIP #78
Manage questions with positive content.

The actual content of your answers should be stated in the positive. Take, for example, the type of hobbies you communicate to employers. Many employers prefer "active" hobbies, such as swimming, tennis, golfing, or jogging, to more sedentary activities, such as reading, stamp collecting, and computer-related activities.

But the most important examples of positive content relate to specific interview questions which are designed to probe your knowledge, abilities, motivations, strengths, and weaknesses. The employer's goal is somewhat negative in the interview; he or she wants to know why **not** to hire you. The major unstated question is *"What are your weaknesses?"* Several other questions may be asked to indirectly answer this major one.

You should always phrase your answers to questions in a positive manner. Avoid the use of such commonly used negatives as *"can't,"* *"didn't,"* and *"wouldn't."* These terms direct listeners into negative avenues of thinking. They do not communicate optimism and enthusiasm – two qualities you should demonstrate in the interview. Take, for example, two different answers to the following interview question:

QUESTION: *Why did you major in business?*

ANSWER 1:   *That's real funny. I wanted to major in history, but my parents told me if they were footing the bills, I shouldn't be studying useless subjects. I tried political science, biology, and accounting but didn't like any of them. Business administration wasn't that difficult for me. I couldn't think of*

> _anything I like more – except perhaps history. And_
> _it's not a bad field to be in these days._

ANSWER 2:   _I always enjoyed business and wanted to make it a_
> _career. As a youth I had my own paper route, sold_
> _books door to door, and was a member of Junior_
> _Achievement. In college I was involved in a couple_
> _of small businesses. It seems as though I have_
> _always been in business. I tend to have a knack for_
> _it, and I love it. My major in business administra-_
> _tion further strengthened my desire to go into_
> _business. It gave me better direction. What I want_
> _is to work with a small and growing firm that_
> _would use my abilities to plan and implement_
> _marketing strategies._

While the first answer may be the more truthful, it presents a negative, immature, and haphazard image of you. The second answer, while also truthful, stresses the positive by communicating strengths, purpose, and enthusiasm.

Let's take as another example an employer who asks the interviewee why she is leaving her present job:

QUESTION: _Why do you want to leave your present job?_

ANSWER 1:   _After working there three years, I don't feel I am_
> _going anywhere. Morale isn't very good, and the_
> _management doesn't reward us according to our_
> _productivity. I really don't like working there_
> _anymore._

ANSWER 2:   _After working there three years, I have learned a_
> _great deal about managing people and developing_
> _new markets. But it is time for me to move on to a_
> _larger and more progressive organization where I_
> _can use my marketing experience in several differ-_
> _ent areas. I am ready to take on more responsibili-_
> _ties. This change will be a positive step in my pro-_
> _fessional growth._

Again, the first answer communicates too many negatives. The second answer is positive and upbeat in its orientation toward skills, accomplishments, and the future.

Most interview questions can be answered by using positive language that further emphasizes that you are competent, intelligent, friendly, spontaneous, honest, and likable. This language should project your strengths, purpose, and enthusiasm. If you feel you need to practice formulating positive responses to interview questions, examine the sample questions outlined in Tip #56 and in the Appendix. Consider alternative positive responses to each question. You also may want your spouse or friend to ask you questions. Tape record the interview and review your responses. Are your answers positive in both form and content? Do they communicate your strengths, purpose, and enthusiasm? Keep practicing the interview until you spontaneously respond with positive yet truthful answers.

TIP #79
Overcome objections and negatives.

Interviewers are likely to have certain objections to hiring you. Some of their objections may be legitimate whereas others are misunderstandings. Objections might relate to illegal questions concerning marital status, religion, or age. But many objections are perfectly legal and are common ways of distinguishing one candidate from another. Among these objections are questions relating to your bona fide qualifications – education, experience, and skills.

If you are weak in any of the qualification areas, you may not be able to overcome the objections unless you acquire the necessary qualifications. But chances are these qualifications have been screened prior to the interview and thus will not be a topic of discussion. If, on the other hand, your education, experience, and skill level pose any objections in the mind of the interviewer, stress again your strengths in a positive and enthusiastic manner. Objections to your educational background will be the easiest to deal with if your experience and skills demonstrate your value.

On the other hand, one objection individuals increasingly encounter today from employers is being **over-qualified**. More and more people by choice are moving **down** in their careers rather than up. Given the desire for, and ease of, higher education, more and more people appear over-educated for many jobs today.

Employers' objections to candidates being over-qualified are a legitimate concern. From the perspective of employers, the over-qualified individual may quickly become a liability. Becoming unhappy with the job, they leave after a short period of time. Other individuals may have an unrealistic ambition of quickly moving up the organizational ladder. In either case, the over-qualified individual may cost an employer more than he or she is worth.

On the other hand, the over-qualified candidate may think he or she is doing the employer a favor – the company is getting more for their money. If this is your perception of your value, you need to change it immediately. Unless you are prepared to take a position which is beneath your qualifications and can clearly communicate your desire to the employer so as to lessen his or her fears, you will most likely not get the job. In the interview you must convince the employer that you understand his or her apprehension about you, but you are willing, able, and eager to do the job.

While you want to communicate your strengths, employers want to know your weaknesses. There are several ways to handle questions that try to get at your weaknesses. If the interviewer frankly asks you, *"What are some of your weaknesses?,"* be prepared to give him or her positive responses. You can do this in any of four different ways:

1. Discuss a negative unrelated to the job being considered:

I don't enjoy accounting. I know it's important, but I find it boring. Even at home my wife takes care of our books. Marketing is what I like to do. Other people are better at bookkeeping than I am. I'm glad this job doesn't involve accounting!

2. Discuss a negative which can also be a positive:

I'm somewhat of a workaholic. I love my work, but I sometimes don't spend enough time with my family. I've been going into the office seven days a week, and I often put in 12-hour days. I'm now learning to better manage my time. I've created better balance in my life and with my family.

3. Discuss a negative which the interviewer already knows:

I spent a great deal of time working on advanced degrees, as indicated in my resume, and thus I lack extensive work experience. However, I believe my education has prepared me well for this job. My leadership experience in college taught me how to work with people, organize, and solve problems. I write well and quickly. My research experience helped me analyze, synthesize, and develop strategies.

4. Discuss a negative which you have improved upon:

I used to get over-committed and miss important deadlines. But then I read a book on time management and learned what I was doing wrong. Within three weeks I reorganized my use of time and found I could meet my deadlines with little difficulty. The quality of my work also improved. Now I have time to work out at the gym each day. I'm doing more and feeling better at the same time.

Part of the analysis of your audience – the interviewer – may include determining what concerns the employer may have about you, but may not ask. For example, if you are retired and decide to pursue a second career, you may expect some employers to be hesitant to hire you. Some of their concerns might include your health: would you be out a lot because of illness? Or your ability to fit into a new work environment: would it be difficult for you to take direction from someone younger than you – especially if you had been a senior level manager in your pre-retirement position? Anticipate concerns you believe the interviewer may have but be reluctant to raise. It may be to your advantage to raise them – especially if you are able to put a positive spin on the situation.

TIP #80
Handle silence positively.

Many people feel uncomfortable with silence and treat silence as if it were an enemy. It can be your worst enemy if your response is to fill the silence and you begin rambling on about anything in order to fill the space.

Be careful of silence. There may be a pause because the interviewer is considering a remark you just made or is deciding on the next question. The pause may be intentional on the part of the interviewer to see how you will handle yourself. Will you be comfortable with the silence or will you try to fill it with whatever comes to mind? You have two choices that are positive ones for your candidacy. You may keep silent and wait for the interviewer to continue, or you might ask the interviewer if he would like to know more about _____. Of course _____ is an area of strength that you welcome an opportunity to talk about. If you choose the second option, keep your comments focused and relatively short.

TIP #81
Delay salary considerations as long as possible.

Usually salary is brought up by the interviewer near the end of the first interview, during a second or third interview, or after a job offer has been made. However, some interviewers will bring it up earlier. It is almost always to your advantage to delay discussion of salary as long as possible. In the meantime, you need to do two things:

- Determine the **worth** of the position.

- Demonstrate your **value** to the employer.

You can only do these two things **after** you have had a chance to interview for the position – not at the beginning or in the middle of the interview. You need to have the opportunity to determine what the job is worth based on the duties and responsibilities of the position – something you can best evaluate after you have a chance to ask questions about the position. You also want the opportunity to promote your value to the employer during the give and take of the interview.

Interviewers who bring up salary early – during a telephone screening interview or early in the initial interview – are usually trying to screen people out of consideration based on salary expectations that are either too high or even too low! Attempt to stall by indicating that salary is "open" or that you need to know more about the position before you can discuss salary.

8

Ask Thoughtful Questions

W HILE MOST CANDIDATES ARE primarily concerned with giving appropriate answers to anticipated interview questions, few actually prepare to ask questions of their own. Most have nothing to say, or they respond with this statement when the interviewer closes by asking *"Do you have any questions?"*:

No, you seemed to have covered everything.

Such a response does nothing to enhance the interviewee's candidacy. Indeed, it indicates a possible lack of interest in the position and an eagerness to leave as soon as possible.

Employers increasingly report that it's often the quality of a candidate's **questions** – not answers – that was critical in making the final hiring decision.

In this chapter we outline a few tips on how you can best ask thoughtful questions that will both generate useful information for making your own decisions and impress the interviewer by indicating your interest in the position and your competence in doing the job.

TIP #82
Respond to sensitive questions with facts,
a compelling story, and redirection questions.

There will be times during a job interview when you feel uneasy about certain questions or unsure if the answers you are giving are sufficient to satisfy the interviewer. At those moments, it's a good idea to start asking questions that will (1) redirect the conversation or (2) bring greater clarity to the subject. For example, if you are asked about a potential red flag in your background, such as frequently changing jobs (*"Why have you had so many different unrelated jobs during the past seven years?"*), try to redirect the question by making a central statement followed by a personal story and related questions:

1. **Make a statement that sets the stage for your "story"**

   Seven years ago I was both clueless and careerless. Not knowing what I really wanted to do, I kept going from one dead-end job to another. I was unhappy with my life. I knew I had to do something else, but I didn't know what it was nor how to change my life.

2. **Tell a compelling story of self-transformation**

   Three years ago I read about this new two-year cybersecurity certificate program at Delta Community College. It really caught my interest since I love computers and have always wanted to do investigative work, but not with a police department or a government agency. I thought this may be the perfect combination for a career. So I enrolled in the program and discovered that indeed it was what I really wanted to do for a career. I initially enrolled as a part-time student because of my work schedule. I had difficulty getting evening courses since this was primarily a daytime program for full-time students. After the first semester I knew it would take me a few years to complete the program as a part-time student. So I decided to quit my job and took several part-time jobs at night. I'm glad I made those job changes because they enabled me to complete the program within two years.

3. **Ask questions to redirect the conversation around your goals and competencies and the employer's hiring needs.**

> *Is there anything more you would like to know about this period in my life?*

> *Would you like more information about those jobs, even though they don't directly relate to my recent training and goals?*

> *I would love to tell you more about how my cybersecurity training has prepared me for this job. Could I share some of my experiences with you on how I might be able to deal with a few of your major client issues? I have ideas that relate to a new security management software program that has attracted many new clients to other companies.*

If you feel uncomfortable answering a question, you might ask for clarification or redirect the conversation line by asking one of these questions:

> *I'm not sure if that's exactly what you are looking for. Is there something else I could share with you along these same lines?*

> *That's a brief summary. Would you like more details, or did I give you enough information on that issue?*

> *I have lots of other good examples related to how I solved those problems. Would you like me to share another one with you, or was that one sufficient?*

Tip #83
Prepare a list of questions you need to ask.

In preparation for the job interview, you should outline questions you want to ask the prospective employer. You need to ask questions to elicit information about the position and organization; indeed, you want to know if the position is fit for you. In addition, the interviewer will be making judgments about your interests, qualifications, personality, and competence based on the number and types of questions you ask.

What types of questions should you ask in order to get information and impress the interviewer? In general, questions relating to job duties, responsibilities, opportunities for training, and employee advancement within the company are appropriate. Avoid asking self-centered questions, especially any dealing with salary and benefits.

In addition to some of the questions suggested in Tip #67, you may want to ask the following questions. Again, do not consider this to be an exhaustive list, but use it to generate additional questions appropriate for your situation:

- *What duties and responsibilities does the job entail?*
- *Where does this position fit into the organization?*
- *Is this a new position?*
- *What are you looking for in a successful candidate?*
- *When was the last person promoted?*
- *Is this position vacant now? Why? For how long?*
- *What is the best experience and background for this position?*
- *What expectations do you have for this position long-term?*
- *Whom would I report to? Tell me a little about these people. Are you happy with them? What are their strengths and weaknesses?*
- *What is the most difficult challenge the person will face in this position?*
- *May I talk with present and previous employees about this job and organization?*
- *What problems might I expect to encounter on this job? (efficiency, quality control, declining profits, internal politics, evaluation)*
- *What has been done recently in regards to _____ ?*
- *How did you get your job?*
- *How long have you been with this company?*
- *Tell me about promotions and advancement with this company.*
- *What are your expectations from the person hired for this job?*

Having prepared a written list of questions, many interviewees wonder whether they should memorize them or write them down and take them to the interview. We suggest writing them on an index card and carrying the card in your suit pocket, attaché case, or purse.

Tip #84
Wait for an appropriate time to ask questions.

Let the interviewer start the interview and ask his questions. In the process of answering questions, you should ask a few questions to clarify points and redirect the line of questioning. Keep these questions to a minimum since you don't want to dominate the conversation with your questions and thus frustrate the interviewer, who may feel he can't get a word in edgewise.

Once the interviewer has exhausted his list of questions, he'll probably turn to you and ask if you have any questions. This will be your time to focus on several key questions. Use this time wisely.

Tip #85
When asked if you have any questions,
refer to your prepared list.

If, as the interview progresses, you remember all the questions you wished to ask without reference to the card, that is excellent. On the other hand, you may find you simply can't recall those questions – especially given the stress of the situation. If that happens, mention to the interviewer that you have some questions you want to be sure you don't forget to ask, and then refer to your index card. By formulating questions prior to the interview, you demonstrate concern about the position as well as preparation for the interview. Most interviewers will view you in a positive manner if you do this.

Tip #86
Focus on acquiring useful information
about the organization, position, job,
and people you'll be working with.

Remember your primary goal at the job interview – to acquire useful information in order to make a well-informed decision about your career future. If you get distracted and become too hungry for the position, you may not ask the right questions for making a good decision. Stay on message: every question should be designed to elicit useful information about the organization, position, job performance, and people you will be working with. There is nothing worse than to accept a job and then learn within the first week that you probably made a bad decision, especially after learning you are working with a real jerk of a boss who has a track record for burning out new employees within three months! You'll then ask yourself this belated question:

> *Why didn't I ask more questions about this organization, position, job, and the people I would be working with? I can't believe I came into this job having asked so few questions about what I was getting into!*

Tip #87
Make your questions inclusive.

Try to be as inclusive as possible when asking and answering questions. Rather than talk about "I", "me", "you," or "the company," interject the notion that you have already been hired and are working with the individual by talking about "we." For example, compare the following statements:

> *What would **I** be expected to accomplish during the first six months?*
> *What would be **our** goals during the first six months?*
> *How would **you** solve that problem?*
> *How would **we** solve that problem?*

By using such inclusive terminology, you subtly plant the idea that you are part of the team. In other words, you've been hired!

Tip #88
Focus on the employer and organization.

Make sure your questions primarily focus on the employer and organization rather than on your needs. Going beyond the more position-focused questions in Tip #83, you should ask broader questions about the company:

- *Can you tell me more about the major challenges facing this company?*

- *Where do you see the company five years from now?*

- *How does this position fit into your future plans?*

- *Can you tell me about your experiences with this company? What do you especially enjoy about working here?*

- *What do other employees especially like about this company?*

- *Who do you see as your major competitors?*

- *Whom would you recommend as a good role model?*

- *What type of person do you see as the ideal for this position? What qualities and characteristics would this person have?*

- *Do you have an organizational chart that would give me a good idea as to how this position fits into the larger organization?*

- *How do you measure success and performance in this company?*

- *What is the one thing you feel the company needs to do in the next year to improve its performance?*

When you ask such employer-centered questions, you impress upon the interviewer the following qualities:

1. You are interested in the position.
2. You are concerned about the company.
3. You have an inquisitive mind.
4. You can initiate a focused conversation.
5. You take initiative and show leadership qualities.
6. You confront issues in high-risk situations.

Tip #89
Show your attitude and enthusiasm.

When asking questions, try to communicate the same qualities we recommended for answering questions (Tip #3) – a positive attitude and a high level of enthusiasm and energy. Employers want to hire individuals who exude such qualities. Avoid questions that suggest negative thinking, and always use positive form and content (Tips #76 and #78) when asking questions.

Tip #90
Avoid asking questions about compensation and benefits.

As we noted in Tip #81, you should avoid asking self-centered questions. None are more self-centered than salary and benefit questions. Indeed, questions dealing with salary and benefits should be avoided during initial interviews or early stages of the interview unless they are raised first by the interviewer. Of course you are interested in salary, but you do not want to create the impression it is your primary concern. Remember, the prospective employer is interested in what **benefits** you will bring to the organization. At the same time, you need to **establish your value** in the eyes of the employer prior to discussing money.

Tip #91
Be careful in asking too many questions at the first interview.

While it's important to ask questions at the job interview, be judicious in limiting the number of questions you ask during the first interview. Ask just enough broad questions, such as those in Tip #88, to satisfy your curiosity about the organization. Avoid becoming an irritating inquisitor who may appear to be "more trouble that you are worth" – you talk too much about sensitive matters. Always keep in mind that you have been invited to the job interview. Let the interviewer dominate the stage. You can always ask other more detailed questions (Tip #83) in subsequent job interviews with this employer.

9

Remember to Close and Follow Up

W HAT DO YOU PLAN TO DO when the interview is over? When is it really over? Beyond answering and asking questions, what other actions can you take to influence the outcome of the interview?

In this chapter we reveal a variety of tips that relate to two of the most important, yet neglected, phases of the job interview – close and follow up. If you want to get invited back to another interview and offered the job, you must engage in certain close and follow-up activities.

TIP #92
Close by summarizing and restating your interest in the job.

Interviewers normally will initiate the close by standing, shaking hands, and thanking you for coming to the interview. They may express some variation of *"Glad you could come by today. We have several other candidates to interview. We'll be in touch."* In response, most interviewees shake hands, thank the interviewer, leave, and hope for the best. Don't do this!

Hope is not a good job search strategy.

At this stage, you should summarize the interview in terms of your interests, strengths, and goals. Briefly restate your qualifications and continuing interest in working with the employer. For example, an accountant might summarize as follows:

> _I'm really glad I had the chance to talk with you. I know, with what I learned when I reorganized the accounting department at XYZ Corporation, I could increase your profits, too._

TIP #93
Don't play competitive games.

Anxious to receive a job offer at the end of the interview, some candidates feel compelled to interject an element of competition into the closing of the interview by indicating they either have, or expect to soon receive an offer from another company. If this is true and you are under pressure to make a decision, let this employer know about your time-sensitive situation. You might say the following:

> _I want to let you know that I've received a job offer from another company that is expecting me to make a decision within the next two days. Is there any chance you could let know your decision by Thursday? I really prefer this job, but I need to soon respond to the offer._

If you are only interviewing with other companies and have not received a job offer, avoid playing the hard-to-get game. It would be dishonest for you to indicate you have a job offer when in fact you do not. Trying to put pressure on the employer to quickly offer you the job could backfire – the employer may decide to "let you go."

TIP #94
Ask for the job if you really want it.

One of the most effective closings is to simply ask for the job. In fact, employers want to hire candidates who are enthusiastic about their company and who want to work with them. You can ask for the job in several different ways. The following examples are designed to help you formulate a close that best fits your situation:

Even though I'm looking at other opportunities, this is really the place I would love to work. It's where I know I can make a difference.

I'll be very disappointed if you don't hire me! This is the place where I really want to build both a company and a career.

I've always dreamt of working in such an innovative company where employees are considered family. If you offer me the job, I can guarantee within six months you'll see a big change in your bottom line.

TIP #95
Ask for permission to follow up.

Ask the interviewer when he or she expects to make the hiring decision. If the response is *"Friday of next week,"* then ask, *"If I haven't heard by the following Monday, may I give you a call?"* Almost everyone will say you may, and you will have solved your problem of wondering when you will hear about the final decision and what to do next.

If you haven't heard anything by the time the designated Monday arrives, do call. Some interviewers use this technique to see if you will follow through with a call – others are just inconsiderate.

By taking the initiative in this manner, the employer will be prompted to clarify your status soon, and you will have an opportunity to talk again.

TIP #96
Be prepared to give the interviewer a list of professional and personal references.

Many interviewers will ask you for a list of references. Be sure to prepare such a list **prior to** the interview. Include the names, addresses, and phone numbers of four individuals who will give you positive professional and personal recommendations. If asked for references, you will appear well prepared by presenting a list in this manner. If you fail to prepare this information ahead of time, you may appear at best disorganized and at worst lacking good references. Always anticipate being asked for specific names, addresses, and phone numbers of your references.

TIP #97
Make follow-up a top priority.

Follow-up is a much neglected art, but it is the key to unlocking employ-ers' doors and for achieving job search success. But many people fear following up. Like giving a speech, it requires initiating communications with strangers! Unfortunately, many interviewees would rather wait to hear from the employer than to take actions that could influence the final hiring decision.

Follow-up occurs at the implementation stage of your job search. Without an effective follow-up campaign, you may be passed over for the job. If you want interviewers to know that you are interested in their position, you need to follow up with a nice thank-you letter and/or phone call, in which you restate your strongest talents. At this stage, timing is everything.

TIP #98
Send a thank-you letter.

Shortly after the interview – later the same day or the next day at the latest – send a thank-you letter by mail and/or e-mail. In this letter:

1. Express your appreciation for the time the interviewer(s) spent with you

2. Indicate your continued interest in the position.

3. Restate any special skills or experience you would bring to the job (keep this brief and well focused).

4. Close by mentioning that you will call in a few days to inquire about the employer's decision.

If you choose to mail the letter, remember that this is a business letter and the stationery, format, and writing style should reflect your profes-sionalism. The letter should be typed – not handwritten – on good quality bond paper. Page 138 includes an example of such a thank-you letter. For additional examples of such letters, see our companion volumes, *Nail the Cover Letter!* and *201 Dynamite Job Search Letters*.

Thank-You Letter
Post-Job Interview

2962 Forrest Drive
Denver, Colorado 82171
May 28, 20 ____

Thomas F. Harris
Director, Personnel Department
Coastal Products Incorporated
7229 Lakewood Drive
Denver, Colorado 82170

Dear Mr. Harris:

Thank you again for the opportunity to interview for the marketing position. I appreciated your hospitality and enjoyed meeting you and members of your staff.

The interview convinced me of how compatible my background, interest, and skills are with the goals of Coastal Products Incorporated. My prior marketing experience with the Department of Commerce has prepared me to take a major role in developing both domestic and international marketing strategies. I am confident my work for you will result in increased profits within the first two years.

As you suggested, I'll give you a call Thursday afternoon to see if you've made a decision. In the meantime, if you have any additional questions, please let me know. I look forward to meeting you again, hopefully as a member of your team.

Sincerely,

Tim Potter

Tim Potter
pottert@mymail.com

TIP #99
Follow through with a telephone call when the decision date has passed.

Remember (Tip #95) at the end of the interview you asked when a decision would be made, and asked whether you could call if you hadn't heard within a couple of days of that date? Don't just ask the question and leave it at that – you must follow through. If the decision date has passed, make the follow-up call.

If no decision has yet been made, your call will remind them of your continued interest. You also should impress the employer as someone who does follow through, and he could expect this same commitment from you as an employee. If the employer has made a decision and was about to call and offer you the position, that's great! If someone else has been offered the job you may be disappointed, but it is just as well to find out now and concentrate your job search efforts elsewhere than to waste time waiting to hear about this job.

10

Get the Offer, Then
Talk Money to Power

I N THE END, YOU WANT to get a job offer and then receive fair
compensation for your talent. However, many job seekers make
several salary mistakes, from not knowing their worth and prematurely discussing salary to failing to properly negotiate a compensation package that truly reflects their value in today's job market. Part of
the problem is cultural – reluctance to talk about money and other
people's salaries. But the major problem relates to the lack of compensation information and weak salary negotiation skills.

The tips in this chapter introduce you to the major issues relating to
salary and job offers. For more information on how to become a savvy
salary negotiator, see our three companion volumes: *Dynamite Salary
Negotiations*, *Salary Negotiation Tips for Professionals*, and *Get a
Raise in 7 Days*.

TIP #100
Approach most salaries as negotiable.

Contrary to what many job seekers believe, salary is seldom predeter-
mined except for entry-level positions. Most employers have some flexibility to negotiate salary or benefits. While most employers do not try to

exploit applicants, neither do they want to pay applicants more than what they have to or what a candidate will accept.

Salaries are usually assigned to positions or jobs rather than to individuals. But not everyone is of equal value in performing the job; some are more productive than others. Since individual performance differs, you should attempt to establish your value in the eyes of the employer rather than accept a salary figure for the job. The art of salary negotiation will help you do this.

TIP #101
Become a savvy salary negotiator.

Just how savvy a salary negotiator are you? How prepared are you to negotiate a salary that truly reflects your worth? What knowledge and skills do you need to become a savvy salary negotiator?

Let's start by evaluating your knowledge and skill level for becoming an effective salary negotiator. Respond to the following statements by circling "Yes" or "No." If you are uncertain about your answer, just leave the statement alone and move on to the next statement.

1. I know what I'm worth in comparison
   to others in today's job market.   Yes   No

2. I know what others make in my company.   Yes   No

3. I can negotiate a salary 15 percent higher
   than my current salary.   Yes   No

4. I can negotiate a salary 5-10 percent higher
   than what the employer is prepared to offer me. Yes   No

5. I know where I can quicky find salary
   information for my particular position.   Yes   No

6. I usually feel comfortable talking about
   compensation issues with others, including
   my boss.   Yes   No

7. I understand the different types of stock
   options and equity incentives offered by
   employers in my field.   Yes   No

8. I'm familiar with how various compensation options work with most employers, such as signing bonuses, performance bonuses, cafeteria plans, reimbursement accounts, disability insurance, 401k plans, SEPs, CODAs, stock options, flex-time, tuition reimbursements, and severance pay.   Yes   No

9. I know what my current compensation package is worth when translated into dollar equivalents.   Yes   No

10. I'm prepared to negotiate more than seven different compensation options.   Yes   No

11. I have a list of at least 50 accomplishments and a clear pattern of performance which I can communicate to prospective employers.   Yes   No

12. I'm prepared to tell at least five different one- to three-minute stories about my proudest professional achievements.   Yes   No

13. If asked to state my "salary requirements" in a cover letter or on an application, I know what to write.   Yes   No

14. I know when I should and should not discuss salary during an interview.   Yes   No

15. I know what to say if the interviewer asks me, *"What are your salary expectations?"*   Yes   No

16. I know what questions to ask during the interview in order to get information about salaries in the interviewer's company.   Yes   No

17. I know when it's time to stop talking and start serious negotiations.   Yes   No

18. I know how to use the "salary range" to create "common ground" and strengthen my negotiation position.   Yes   No

19. I know how to use silence to strengthen my negotiation position.   Yes   No

20. If offered a position, I know what to
    say and do next.   Yes   No

If you responded "No" to more than three of the above statements or "Yes" to fewer than 15 of the statements, you need to work on developing your salary negotiation skills.

TIP #102
Avoid 21 salary negotiation mistakes

Job seekers typically make several salary negotiation errors, which often result in knocking them out of consideration for the job or they receive and accept a lower salary than what they could have gotten had they practiced a few of the salary tips outlined in this chapter. Several of these errors also may leave a bad impression with an employer – that you have a poor attitude, or you are basically a self-centered job seeker who primarily focuses on salary and benefits rather than on the performance needs of the employer and organization. The most frequent errors you should avoid include:

1. Engage in wishful thinking – believing you are worth a lot more than you are currently being paid but having no credible evidence to support this belief.

2. Approach the job search as an exercise in being clever and manipulative rather than being clear, correct, and competent in communicating your value to others.

3. Fail to research salary options and comparables and thus having few supports to justify your worth.

4. Fail to compile a list of specific accomplishments, including anecdotal one- to three-minute performance stories, that provide evidence of your value to employers.

5. Reveal salary expectations on the resume or in a letter.

6. Answer the question *"What are your salary requirements?"* before being offered the job.

7. Raise the salary question rather than waiting for the employer to do so.

8. Fail to ask questions about the company, job, and previous occupants of the position.

9. Ask *"Is this offer negotiable?"*

10. Quickly accept the first offer, believing that's what the position is really worth and that an employer might be offended if you try to negotiate.

11. Accept the offer on the spot.

12. Accept the offer primarily because of compensation.

13. Try to negotiate compensation during the first interview.

14. Forget to calculate the value of benefits and thus only focus on the gross salary figure.

15. Focus on benefits, stock options, and perks rather than on the gross salary figure.

16. Negotiate a salary figure rather discuss a salary range.

17. Negotiate over the telephone or by e-mail.

18. Talk too much and listen too little.

19. Focus on your needs rather than the employer's needs.

20. Try to play "hardball."

21. Express a negative attitude toward the employer's offer.

TIP #103
Avoid discussing salary before being offered the job.

Employers often raise the salary question early in the interview. They may actually do this during a telephone screening interview. Their basic goal is to either screen you into or out of consideration for the position on salary criteria. Like stating your salary expectations on a resume or in a cover letter, responding to this question with a figure early in the interview puts you at a disadvantage. The old poker saying that *"He who reveals his hand first is at a disadvantage"* is especially true when negotiating salary. Time should work in your favor. After all, you need more information about the job and your responsibilities in order to determine the value of the position. What is the job really worth? A job worth $70,000

*Salary should be the very last thing you talk about – **after** you receive a job offer.*

a year has different levels of responsibility than one worth only $30,000 a year. If the employer raises the salary expectation questions early in the interview, it's best to respond by saying *"I really need to know more about the position and my responsibilities before I can discuss compensation. Can you tell me about . . . ?"* This response will usually result in postponing the salary question and impress upon the employer that you are a thoughtful professional who is more employer-centered than self-centered with your interest in the position. Salary should be the very last thing you talk about – within the context of a job offer, which may not occur during the first interview. Once you have been offered the job, then talk about compensation.

TIP #104
Let the employer volunteer salary information.

Today, many candidates go through three to seven interviews with an employer before receiving a job offer. Except for some entry-level positions, the first interview seldom deals with the money question, although this question can arise at any time to screen someone into or out of consideration. You should never raise the salary issue, for to do so puts you at a disadvantage. Expect the salary offer, and accompanying salary negotiations, to take place during the final interview. The signal that you should talk seriously about money is when you are offered the job. The offer comes first followed by discussion of appropriate compensation. Another way of handling the *"What are your salary requirements?"* question is to respond by asking, *"Are you offering me the position?"* If the response is *"No,"* then you might respond by saying, *"I really need to know more about the position and your company before I feel comfortable discussing compensation."* Alternatively, you might want to use this occasion to do research on the company's salary structure by asking, *"By the way, how much are you paying at present for this position?"* Always try to get the employer to volunteer salary information from which you can formulate your response.

TIP #105
Look at the total compensation package.

One of the easiest ways to survey your compensation options and assign value to your ideal compensation package is to use the following checklist of compensation options. Consider each item and then value it by assigning a dollar amount. When finished, add up the total dollars assigned to get a complete picture of the value of your present or past compensation package.

Element	Value
Basic Compensation Issues	
❑ Base salary	$ _____
❑ Commissions	$ _____
❑ Corporate profit sharing	$ _____
❑ Personal performance bonuses/incentives	$ _____
❑ Cost of living adjustment	$ _____
❑ Overtime	$ _____
❑ Signing bonus	$ _____
❑ Cash in lieu of certain benefits	$ _____
Health Benefits	
❑ Medical insurance	$ _____
❑ Dental insurance	$ _____
❑ Vision insurance	$ _____
❑ Prescription package	$ _____
❑ Life insurance	$ _____

❑ Accidental death and disability insurance $ _____
❑ Evacuation insurance (international travel) $ _____

Vacation and Time Issues

❑ Vacation time $ _____
❑ Sick days $ _____
❑ Personal time $ _____
❑ Holidays $ _____
❑ Flex-time $ _____
❑ Compensatory time $ _____
❑ Paternity/maternity leave $ _____
❑ Family leave $ _____

Retirement-Oriented Benefits

❑ Defined benefit plan $ _____
❑ 401(k) plan $ _____
❑ Deferred compensation $ _____
❑ Savings plans $ _____
❑ Stock-purchase plans $ _____
❑ Stock bonus $ _____
❑ Stock options $ _____
❑ Ownership/equity $ _____

Education

❑ Professional continuing education $ _____
❑ Tuition reimbursement for you or your
  family members $ _____

Military

❑ Compensatory pay during active duty $ _____
❑ National Guard $ _____

Perquisites

❑ Cellular phone $ _____
❑ Company car or vehicle/mileage allowance $ _____
❑ Expense accounts $ _____
❑ Liberalization of business-related expenses $ _____
❑ Child care $ _____
❑ Cafeteria privileges $ _____
❑ Executive dining room privileges $ _____
❑ First-class hotels $ _____
❑ First-class air travel $ _____

❑ Upgrade business travel $ _____
❑ Personal use of frequent-flyer awards $ _____
❑ Convention participation: professionally related $ _____
❑ Parking $ _____
❑ Paid travel for spouse $ _____
❑ Professional association memberships $ _____
❑ Athletic club memberships $ _____
❑ Social club memberships $ _____
❑ Use of company-owned facilities $ _____
❑ Executive office $ _____
❑ Office with a window $ _____
❑ Laptop computers $ _____
❑ Private secretary $ _____
❑ Portable fax $ _____
❑ Employee discounts $ _____
❑ Incentive trips $ _____
❑ Sabbaticals $ _____
❑ Discounted buying club memberships $ _____
❑ Free drinks and meals $ _____

Relocation Expenses

❑ Direct moving expenses $ _____
❑ Moving costs for unusual property $ _____
❑ Trips to find suitable housing $ _____
❑ Loss on sale of present home
     or lease termination $ _____
❑ Company handling sale of present home $ _____
❑ Housing cost differential between cities $ _____
❑ Mortgage rate differential $ _____
❑ Mortgage fees and closing costs $ _____
❑ Temporary dual housing $ _____
❑ Trips home during dual residency $ _____
❑ Real estate fees $ _____
❑ Utilities hookup $ _____
❑ Drapes/carpets $ _____
❑ Appliance installation $ _____
❑ Auto/pet shipping $ _____
❑ Signing bonus for incidental expenses $ _____
❑ Additional meals expense account $ _____
❑ Bridge loan while owning two homes $ _____
❑ Outplacement assistance for spouse $ _____

Home Office Options

❑ Personal computer $ _____
❑ Internet access $ _____

❑ Copier $ _____
❑ Printer $ _____
❑ Financial planning assistance $ _____
❑ Separate phone line $ _____
❑ Separate fax line $ _____
❑ CPA/tax assistance $ _____
❑ Incidental/support office functions $ _____
❑ Office supplies $ _____
❑ Furniture and accessories $ _____

Severance Packages (Parachutes)

❑ Base salary $ _____
❑ Bonuses/incentives $ _____
❑ Non-compete clause $ _____
❑ Stock/equity $ _____
❑ Outplacement assistance $ _____
❑ Voice mail access $ _____
❑ Statement (letter) explaining why you left $ _____
❑ Vacation reimbursement $ _____
❑ Health benefits or reimbursements $ _____
❑ 401(k) contributions $ _____

TOTAL | $ |

TIP #106
Focus on salary ranges.

Savvy salary negotiators always talk about "salary ranges" rather than specific salary figures. They do so because ranges give them flexibility to negotiate. If, for example, the employer reveals his hand first by saying the job pays $75,000 a year, you could counter by putting the employer's figure at the bottom of your range – *"Based on my salary research as well as my experience, I was expect-*

> *Establish common ground from which to negotiate the figure upwards toward the high end of the range.*

ing between $75,000 and $85,000 a year." By doing this, you **establish common ground** from which to negotiate the figure upwards toward the high end of your range. While the employer may not want to pay more than $75,000, he or she at least knows you are within budget. The employer most likely will counter by saying, *"Well, we might be able to go $78,000."* You, in turn, can counter by saying *"Is it possible to go*

$81,000?" As you will quickly discover in the salary negotiation business, anything is "possible" if you handle the situation professionally – with supports and flexibility. In this situation, you might be able to negotiate a $6,000 increase over the employer's initial offer because you establish common ground with a salary range and then move the employer toward the upper end of your range because you had supports and professional appeal.

TIP #107
Carefully examine benefits.

Many employers will try to impress candidates with the benefits offered by the company. These might include retirement, bonuses, stock options, medical and life insurance, and cost of living adjustments. If the employer includes these benefits in the salary negotiations, do not be overly impressed. Most benefits are standard – they come with the job. When negotiating salary, it is best to talk about specific dollar figures. But don't neglect to both calculate and negotiate benefits according to the checklist on pages 146-149. Benefits can translate into a significant portion of one's compensation, especially if you are offered stock options, profit sharing, pensions, insurance, and reimbursement accounts. Indeed, many individuals in the 1990s who took stock options in lieu of high salaries with start-up high tech firms discovered the importance of benefits when their benefits far out weighed their salaries; making only $30,000 a year, some of them became instant millionaires when their companies went public! In fact, the U.S. Department of Labor estimates that benefits now constitute 43 percent of total compensation for the average worker. For example, a $60,000 offer with Company X may translate into a compensation package worth $80,000; but a $50,000 offer with Company Y may actually be worth more than $100,000 when you examine their different benefits.

If the salary offered by the employer does not meet your expectations, but you still want the job, you might try to negotiate for some benefits which are not considered standard. These might include longer paid vacations, some flex-time, and profit sharing.

TIP #108
Avoid playing hard-to-get and other
unprofessional closing games.

If you get a job offer but you are considering other employers, let the others know you have a job offer. Telephone them to inquire about your status as well as inform them of the job offer. Sometimes this will prompt employers to make a hiring decision sooner than anticipated. In addition you will be informing them that you are in demand; they should seriously consider you before you get away!

Some job seekers play a bluffing game by telling employers they have alternative job offers even though they don't. Some candidates do this and get away with it. We don't recommend this approach. Not only is it dishonest, it will work to your disadvantage if the employer learns that you were lying. But more important, you should be selling yourself on the basis of your strengths rather than your deceit and greed. If you can't sell yourself honestly, don't expect to get along well on the job. When you compromise your integrity, you demean your value to others and yourself.

TIP #109
Delay accepting an offer until after you
can have had a chance to consider it.

You should accept an offer only after reaching a salary agreement. If you jump at an offer, you may appear needy. Take time to consider your options. Remember, you are committing your time and effort in exchange for money and status. Is this the job you really want? Take some time to think about the offer before giving the employer a definite answer. But don't play hard-to-get and thereby create ill will with your new employer.

While considering the offer, ask yourself several of the same questions you asked at the beginning of your job search:

- What do I want to be doing five years from now?

- How will this job affect my personal life?

- Do I want to travel?

- Do I know enough about the employer and the future of this organization?

- How have previous occupants of this position fared? Why did they leave?

- Are there other job opportunities that better meet my goals?

Accepting a job is serious business. If you make a mistake, you could be locked into a very unhappy situation for a long time.

If you receive one job offer while considering another, you will be able to compare relative advantages and disadvantages. You also will have some external leverage for negotiating salary and benefits. While you should not play games, let the employer know you have alternative job offers. This communicates that you are in demand, others also know your value, and the employer's price is not the only one in town. Use this leverage to negotiate your salary, benefits, and job responsibilities.

TIP #110
Get the job offer in writing.

You should take notes throughout the salary negotiation session. Jot down pertinent information about the terms of employment. At the end of the session, before you get up to leave, summarize what you understand will be included in the compensation package and show it in outline form to the employer. Make sure both you and the employer understand the terms of employment, including specific elements in the compensation package. If you accept the position, be sure to ask the employer to put the offer in writing, which may be in the form of a letter of agreement. This document should spell out your duties and responsibilities as well as detail how you will be compensated. If your agreement includes incentivized pay, make sure it details exactly how your commissions or bonuses will work – how and when they will be paid, set up, and measured. For example, will you be paid at the end of each quarter or at the end of the year? Do you receive a flat bonus, such as $1,000, or a percentage of the sales from an income stream.

Ask the employer to e-mail or fax you a copy of this document for your review. Let him know you'll get back with him immediately. This document should serve as your employment contract.

Appendix

Questions You May Be Asked

THE FOLLOWING QUESTIONS are frequently asked by interviewers. Indeed, you should be able to predict 95 percent of the questions that are likely to be asked in most interviews. Use this appendix as a handy checklist to prepare for your next interview.

As you plan responses to each question, remember to formulate a **strategy**. You should not try to formulate the exact words you would use and then memorize them. To do this would be a big mistake. At best your answer would likely sound memorized and you would greatly diminish your credibility. At worst, you might forget your memorized response in the middle of your answer!

So consider your answers in terms of basic strategies. What do you hope to convey as you respond to each question? Your goal is to convince the interviewer that you should be offered the job. As you get ready to respond, think in terms of the needs of the employer. How do your goals fit with her business needs? Keep this basic tenet in mind as you formulate your strategies in response to questions you are asked. Try to make time prior to the interview to actually talk through your answers to questions. You may practice answering interview questions (which you have made into a list) posed by a friend or family member or you can read each question and then respond. Practice talking your answers into a tape recorder. Play back the tape and evaluate how you sound.

- Do you exude confidence?
- Do you sound dynamic?
- Do you talk in a conversational style? (rather than your response sounding like a "canned" memorized answer)
- Do you speak without excessive fillers such as *"ah," "and ah," "like,"* and *"you know"*?
- Do you seem believable?
- Do you appear likable?

Try to give your best response to each of the following questions using a tape recorder. Then listen to your recorded responses and critique them.

Each time you talk through an answer, your words will be somewhat different since you have purposely not tried to memorize your response. You have thought through the strategy of your response, the "gist" of the message you want to convey, but you have not attempted to commit a response to memory.

Personality and Motivation

1. Why should we hire you?

2. Are you a self-starter?

3. What is your greatest strength?

4. What is your greatest weakness?

5. What would you most like to improve about yourself?

6. What are some of the reasons for your success?

7. Describe your typical workday.

8. Do you anticipate problems or do you react to them?

9. How do you deal with stressful situations?

10. Do you ever lose your temper?

11. How well do you work under deadlines?

12. What contributions did you make to your last (or present) company?

13. What will you bring to this position that others won't?

14. How well do you get along with your superiors?

15. How well do you get along with your co-workers?

16. How do you manage your subordinates?

17. How do you feel about working with superiors who may have less education than you?

18. Do you prefer working alone or with others?

19. How do others view your work?

20. How do you deal with criticism?

21. Do you consider yourself to be someone who takes greater initiative than others?

22. Do you consider yourself a risk-taker?

23. Are you a good time manager?

24. How important is job security?

25. How do you define success?

26. How do you spend your leisure time?

27. What would be the perfect job for you?

28. What really motivates you to perform on the job?

29. How old are you?

30. What does your spouse think about your career?

31. Are you living with anyone?

32. Do you have many debts?

33. Do you own or rent your home?

34. What social or political organizations do you belong to?

Education and Training

35. Why didn't you go to college?

36. Why didn't you finish college?

37. Why did you select _____ college?

38. Why did you major in _____?

39. What was your minor in school?

40. How did your major relate to the work you have done since graduation?

41. Why weren't your grades better in school?

42. What subjects did you enjoy most?

43. What subjects did you enjoy least?

44. If you could go back and do it over again, what would you change about your college education?

45. What extracurricular activities did you participate in during college?

46. Tell me about your role in (<u>one of your extracurricular activities</u>).

47. What leadership positions did you hold in college?

48. How does your degree prepare you for the job at _____?

49. Did you work part-time or full-time while you were in college?

50. Are you planning to take additional courses or start graduate school over the next year or two?

51. If you had a choice of several short training sessions to attend, which two or three would you select?

52. What materials do you read regularly to keep up with what is going on in your field?

53. What is the most recent skill you have learned?

54. What are your educational goals over the next few years?

Experience and Skills

55. Why do you want to leave your present job or previous jobs?

56. Why have you changed jobs so frequently?

57. Why would you be more likely to stay here?

58. What are your qualifications for this job?

59. What experience prepares you for this job?

60. What did you like most about your present/most recent job?

61. What did you like least about that job?

62. What did you like most about your boss?

63. What did you like least about that boss?

64. Tell me about an ongoing responsibility in your current/most recent job that you enjoyed.

65. How does your present job (or most recent) relate to the overall goals of your department/the company?

66. What has your present/most recent supervisor(s) criticized about your work?

67. What duties in your present/most recent job do you find it difficult to do?

68. Why do you want to leave your present job? Are you being forced out?

69. Why should we hire someone like you – with your experience and motivation?

70. What type of person would you hire for this position?

71. Have you ever been fired or asked to resign?

72. What was the most important contribution you made on your last job?

73. What do you wish you had accomplished in your present/most recent job but were unable to?

74. What is the most important thing you've learned from the jobs you've held?

Career Goals

75. Tell me about yourself.

76. Tell me about your career goals.

77. What would you like to accomplish during the next five years (or ten years).

78. How do your career goals today differ from your career goals five years ago?

79. Where do you see yourself five years from now?

80. Describe a major goal you set for yourself recently?

81. What are you doing to achieve that goal?

82. Have you ever thought of switching careers?

83. How does this job compare to what would be the perfect job for you?

84. What would you change about our company to make this your ideal workplace?

85. How long have you been looking for another job?

Why You Want This Job

86. What do you know about our company?

87. What trends do you see in our industry?

88. Why do you want to work for us?

89. How much business would you bring to our firm?

90. What similarities do you see between this and your current/most recent position?

91. What makes this position different from your current/most recent position?

92. Why are you willing to take a job you are over-qualified for?

93. Why are you willing to take a pay cut from your previous (present position?

94. What would you change about this position?

95. How long would you expect to stay with our company?

96. How do you feel about working overtime or on weekends?

97. Are you willing to relocate?

98. How much are you willing to travel?

99. What are your salary expectations?

100. How soon could you begin work?

101. Do you have any questions?

Unexpected Questions

You may not be asked any questions beyond the ones outlined above. If the questions you are asked do go beyond these, they will most likely fall into one of two categories:

- Specific questions that relate to special knowledge or skills required for the job for which you are being considered.

- Questions that are raised by unusual items or unexplained gaps or omissions on your resume or application.

Look over your resume. Is there anything that stands out? If you spent your junior year abroad – not in Paris or Spain – but in Timbuktu, or your first job was in Inner Mongolia, these points are likely to raise questions simply because they are unusual choices. The interviewer is going to be curious about your experiences as well as what these choices say about you. If you have a two-year unexplained gap in your job history, this gap is bound to raise the question of what you were doing during this time. You need to be ready with honest, yet positive answers, that will further promote your candidacy rather than knock you out of the running.

If you have thoughtfully considered your responses and practiced responding with the gist of the message you want to convey, these questions should not throw you. However, if you haven't given such questions much thought, your responses are likely to show it.

Few questions should ever be answered with just a *"yes"* or *"no."* Remember to provide **examples** as often as possible to support the points you make. If asked by the interviewer whether you are a self-starter you could simply respond *"yes."* However you score few points for this response. It really says nothing except that either you think you are a self-starter or you think this is the response the interviewer wants to hear. But if you follow your *"yes"* response with an example or two of what you did that demonstrates you were a self-starter in your last job (or in college if you have just graduated and have little work experience), you start to sell yourself. You want to impress the interviewer and you want to stand out from the rest of the applicants being interviewed.

Remember to use examples and use them frequently. Examples support assertions about your abilities and thus help sell you to the interviewer. Examples make what you say about your skills and achievements more clear, more interesting, more credible, and more likely to be remembered. They help tell your story.

Behavior- and Situation-Based Questions

Employers are increasingly incorporating behavior-based and situation-based questions in job interviews. As we noted in Chapter 2, "behavior-based" means that the interviewer asks you to describe how you responded when you faced an actual situation. "Hypothetical situational-based" questions don't ask for an actual situation, but ask you to imagine a situation and describe how you would act if that occurred. These types of interview questions are an attempt to get applicants to do what they should be doing anyway: expanding their answers with examples that support the assertions they are making.

Be prepared to respond to these types of open-ended behavior-based and situation-based questions:

1. What would you do if . . .

2. In what situations have you become so involved in the work you were doing that the day flew by?

3. If you were to encounter that same situation now, how would you deal with that person?

4. If you had a choice of working in our department A or department B, which would you choose?

5. Why would you make that choice?

6. Tell me about a recent time when you took responsibility for a task that was outside of our job description.

7. Tell me about a time when you took action without your supervisor's prior approval.

Index

The Authors

OR MORE THAN TWO DECADES Ron and Caryl Krannich have pursued a passion – assisting hundreds of thousands of individuals, from students, the unemployed, and ex-offenders to military personnel, international job seekers, and CEOs, in making critical job and career transitions. Focusing on key job search skills, career changes, and employment fields, their impressive body of work has helped shape career thinking and behavior both in the United States and abroad. Their sound advice has changed numerous lives, including their own!

Ron and Caryl are two of America's leading career and travel writers who have authored more than 80 books. A former Peace Corps Volunteer and Fulbright Scholar, Ron received his Ph.D. in Political Science from Northern Illinois University. Caryl received her Ph.D. in Speech Communication from Penn State University. Together they operate Development Concepts Incorporated, a training, consulting, and publishing firm in Virginia.

The Krannichs are both former university professors, high school teachers, management trainers, and consultants. As trainers and consultants, they have completed numerous projects on management, career development, local government, population planning, and rural development in the United States and abroad. Their career books focus on key job search skills, military and civilian career transitions, government and international careers, ex-offenders and re-entry, travel jobs, and nonprofit organizations. and include such bestselling classics as *High Impact Resumes and Letters, Interview for Success,* and *Change Your Job, Change Your Life,* which continue in print after more than 20 years.

The Krannichs' books represent one of today's most comprehensive collections of career writing. With over 3 million copies in print, their publications are widely available in bookstores, libraries, and career centers. No strangers to the world of Internet employment and travel, they have written *America's Top Internet Job Sites, Haldane's Best Employment Websites for Professionals, The Directory of Websites for International Jobs,* and *Travel Planning on the Internet,* and published several Internet recruitment and job search books. Ron served as the first Work Abroad Advisor to Monster.com. Ron and Caryl also have developed three career-related websites: www.impactpublications.com, www.exoffenderreentry.com, and www.veteransworld.com. Many of their career tips appear on such popular websites as www.monster.com, www.careerbuilder.com, www.campuscareercenter.com, and www.employmentguide.com.

Ron and Caryl live a double life with travel being their best kept *"do what you love"* career secret. Authors of more than 20 travel-shopping guidebooks on various destinations around the world, they continue to pursue their international and travel interests through their innovative *Treasures and Pleasures of . . . Best of the Best* travel-shopping series and related website: www.ishoparoundtheworld.com. When not found at their home and business in Virginia, they are probably somewhere in Europe, Asia, Africa, the Middle East, the South Pacific, the Caribbean, or the Americas following their other passion – researching and writing about quality antiques, arts, crafts, jewelry, hotels, restaurants, and sight-seeing as well as adhering to the career advice they give to others: *"Pursue a passion that enables you to do what you really love to do."* Their passion is best represented on www.ishoparoundtheworld.com.

As both career and travel experts, the Krannichs' work is frequently featured in major newspapers, magazines, and newsletters as well as on radio, television, and the Internet. Available for interviews, consultation, and presentations, they can be contacted as follows:

Ron and Caryl Krannich

krannich@impactpublications.com

Career Resources

THE FOLLOWING CAREER RESOURCES are available directly from Impact Publications. Full descriptions of each title as well as downloadable catalogs, videos, software, games, posters, and related products can be found on our website: www.impact publications.com. Complete this form or list the titles, include shipping (see formula at the end), enclose payment, and send your order to:

IMPACT PUBLICATIONS
9104 Manassas Drive, Suite N
Manassas Park, VA 20111-5211 USA
1-800-361-1055 (orders only)
Tel. 703-361-7300 or Fax 703-335-9486
Email address: query@impactpublications.com
Quick & easy online ordering: www.impactpublications.com

Orders from individuals must be prepaid by check, money order, or major credit card. We accept telephone, fax, and email orders.

Qty.	TITLES	Price	TOTAL
Featured Title			
____	I Can't Believe They Asked Me That!	17.95	_____
Interviews			
____	101 Dynamite Questions to Ask At Your Job Interview	13.95	_____
____	301 Smart Answers to Tough Interview Questions	10.95	_____
____	501+ Great Interview Questions for Employers and the Best Answers for Prospective Employers	24.95	_____
____	Adams Job Interview Almanac	17.95	_____
____	The Best Answer	13.00	_____
____	Don't Blow the Interview	12.95	_____
____	Everything Practice Interview Book	12.95	_____

____ High-Impact Interview Questions	17.95	____
____ Haldane's Best Answers to Tough Interview Questions	15.95	____
____ How to Ace the Brain Teaser Interview	14.95	____
____ Interview for Success	15.95	____
____ Interview Magic	16.95	____
____ Job Interview Tips for People With		
Not-So-Hot Backgrounds	14.95	____
____ Job Interviews for Dummies	16.99	____
____ Job Interviews That Get You Hired	12.95	____
____ KeyWords to Nail Your Job Interview	17.95	____
____ Mastering the Job Interview	19.95	____
____ Mastering the Job Interview and Winning		
the Money Game	12.95	____
____ Monster Careers: Interviewing	15.00	____
____ Nail the Job Interview!	14.95	____
____ Negotiating the Salary	12.95	____
____ Perfect Phases for Negotiating Salary and Job Offers	9.95	____
____ Perfect Phases for the Perfect Interview	9.95	____
____ Pocket Idiot's Guide to Interview Questions and Answers	9.95	____
____ The Savvy Interviewer	10.95	____
____ Sweaty Palms	13.95	____
____ Tell Your Story, Win the Job	19.95	____
____ Win the Interview, Win the Job	15.95	____
____ Winning the Interview Game	12.95	____
____ Winning Job Interviews	12.99	____
____ Winning the Interview Game	12.95	____
____ You Have 3 Minutes!	21.95	____
____ You Got the Interview: Now What?	12.95	____

Salary Negotiations

____ Dynamite Salary Negotiations	15.95	____
____ Get a Raise in 7 Days	14.95	____
____ Negotiating Your Salary	12.95	____
____ Salary Negotiation Tips for Professionals	16.95	____
____ Secrets of Power Salary Negotiating	13.99	____

Attitude and Motivation

____ 100 Ways to Motivate Yourself	14.99	____
____ Attitude Is Everything	14.95	____
____ Change Your Attitude	15.99	____
____ Change Your Thinking, Change Your Life	16.95	____
____ Eat That Frog!	13.95	____
____ Goals!	15.95	____
____ Little Gold Book of YES! Attitude	19.99	____
____ Reinventing Yourself	18.99	____
____ Success Principles	24.95	____

Inspiration and Empowerment

____ 7 Habits of Highly Effective People	15.00	____
____ The 8th Habit	15.00	____
____ 101 Secrets of Highly Effective Speakers	15.95	____
____ Create Your Own Future	24.95	____

____ The Habit Change Workbook	19.95	_____
____ Life Strategies	13.95	_____
____ The Magic of Thinking Big	14.00	_____
____ The Power of Positive Thinking	12.95	_____
____ Power of Purpose	20.00	_____
____ Self Matters	14.00	_____
____ The Story of You	19.99	_____
____ Who Moved My Cheese?	19.95	_____

Testing and Assessment

____ Career Tests	12.95	_____
____ Discover What You're Best At	14.00	_____
____ Do What You Are	18.95	_____
____ Finding Your Perfect Work	16.95	_____
____ I Could Do Anything If Only I Knew What It Was	16.00	_____
____ I Want to Do Something Else, But I'm Not Sure What It Is	15.95	_____
____ Now, Discover Your Strengths	30.00	_____
____ Pathfinder	16.00	_____
____ Smarts	21.95	_____
____ What Should I Do With My Life?	14.95	_____
____ What Type Am I?	14.95	_____
____ What's Your Type of Career?	18.95	_____
____ Who Do You Think You Are?	18.00	_____

Career Exploration and Job Strategies

____ 25 Jobs That Have It All	14.95	_____
____ 40 Best Fields for Your Career	16.95	_____
____ 50 Best Jobs for Your Personality	16.95	_____
____ 50 Cutting Edge Jobs	15.95	_____
____ 95 Mistakes Job Seekers Make and How to Avoid Them	13.95	_____
____ 100 Great Jobs and How to Get Them	17.95	_____
____ 101 Ways to Recession-Proof Your Career	14.95	_____
____ 225 Best Jobs for Baby Boomers	16.95	_____
____ 250 Best Jobs Through Apprenticeships	24.95	_____
____ 300 Best Jobs Without a Four-Year Degree	16.95	_____
____ About.com Guide to Job Searching	17.95	_____
____ America's Top 100 Jobs for People Without a Four-Year Degree	19.95	_____
____ America's Top Jobs for People Re-Entering the Workforce	19.95	_____
____ Best Entry-Level Jobs 2007	16.95	_____
____ Best Jobs for the 21st Century	19.95	_____
____ But What If I Don't Want to Go to College?	16.95	_____
____ Career Change	14.95	_____
____ Change Your Job, Change Your Life	21.95	_____
____ Cool Careers for Dummies	19.99	_____
____ Directory of Executive Recruiters	59.95	_____
____ Five Secrets to Finding a Job	12.95	_____
____ How to Get a Job and Keep It	16.95	_____
____ How to Succeed Without a Career Path	13.95	_____
____ Job Hunting Guide: From College to Career	14.95	_____
____ Job Hunting Tips for People With Hot and Not-So-Hot Backgrounds	17.95	_____

____	Knock 'Em Dead	14.95	____
____	Me, Myself, and I, Inc.	17.95	____
____	No One Will Hire Me!	15.95	____
____	Occupational Outlook Handbook	17.95	____
____	O*NET Dictionary of Occupational Titles	39.95	____
____	Quit Your Job and Grow Some Hair	15.95	____
____	Rites of Passage at $100,000 to $1 Million+	29.95	____
____	Top 300 Careers	18.95	____
____	What Color Is Your Parachute?	17.95	____
____	Your Dream Career for Dummies	16.99	____

Internet Job Search

____	100 Top Internet Job Sites	12.95	____
____	America's Top Internet Job Sites	19.95	____
____	Best Career and Education Websites	12.95	____
____	Career Exploration On the Internet	24.95	____
____	Directory of Websites for International Jobs	19.95	____
____	e-Resumes	16.95	____
____	Guide to Internet Job Searching	15.95	____
____	Haldane's Best Employment Websites for Professionals	15.95	____
____	Job Seeker's Online Goldmine	13.95	____

Resumes and Letters

____	101 Great Tips for a Dynamite Resume	13.95	____
____	201 Dynamite Job Search Letters	19.95	____
____	Adams Cover Letter Almanac	17.95	____
____	Adams Resume Almanac	17.95	____
____	Best KeyWords for Resumes, Cover Letters, & Interviews	17.95	____
____	Best Resumes and CVs for International Jobs	24.95	____
____	Best Resumes for $100,000+ Jobs	24.95	____
____	Best Resumes for People Without a Four-Year Degree	19.95	____
____	Best Cover Letters for $100,000+ Jobs	24.95	____
____	Bioblogs	16.95	____
____	Blue Collar Resume and Job Hunting Guide	15.95	____
____	Competency-Based Resumes	13.99	____
____	Cover Letter Magic	16.95	____
____	Cover Letters for Dummies	16.99	____
____	Cover Letters That Knock 'Em Dead	12.95	____
____	Create Your Digital Portfolio	19.95	____
____	Expert Resumes for Baby Boomers	16.95	____
____	Expert Resumes for Career Changers	16.95	____
____	Expert Resumes for Computer and Web Jobs	16.95	____
____	Expert Resumes for Managers and Executives	16.95	____
____	Expert Resumes for People Returning to Work	16.95	____
____	Gallery of Best Cover Letters	18.95	____
____	Gallery of Best Resumes	18.95	____
____	Haldane's Best Cover Letters for Professionals	15.95	____
____	Haldane's Best Resumes for Professionals	15.95	____
____	High Impact Resumes and Letters	19.95	____
____	Internet Resumes	14.95	____
____	Military Resumes and Cover Letters	21.95	____
____	Nail the Cover Letter!	17.95	____
____	Nail the Resume!	17.95	____

____ Resume Shortcuts	14.95	____
____ Resume, Application, and Letter Tips for People With Hot and Not-So-Hot Backgrounds	17.95	____
____ Resumes for Dummies	16.99	____
____ Resumes That Knock 'Em Dead	12.95	____
____ The Savvy Resume Writer	12.95	____
____ Step-By-Step Resumes	19.95	____
____ Winning Letters That Overcome Barriers to Employment	17.95	____
____ World's Greatest Resumes	14.95	____

Networking

____ Dynamite Telesearch	12.95	____
____ Endless Referrals	16.95	____
____ Fine Art of Small Talk	16.95	____
____ Golden Rule of Schmoozing	12.95	____
____ Great Connections	11.95	____
____ How to Work a Room	14.00	____
____ Little Black Book of Connections	19.95	____
____ Masters of Networking	16.95	____
____ Never Eat Alone	24.95	____
____ One Phone Call Away	24.95	____
____ Power Networking	14.95	____
____ The Savvy Networker	13.95	____
____ Shortcut Your Job Search	12.95	____
____ Work the Pond!	15.95	____

Dress, Image, and Etiquette

____ Business Etiquette for Dummies	21.99	____
____ Dressing Smart for Men	16.95	____
____ Dressing Smart for the New Millennium	15.95	____
____ Dressing Smart for Women	16.95	____
____ Power Etiquette	15.95	____
____ You've Only Got Three Seconds	15.00	____

Military in Transition

____ Expert Resumes for Military-to-Civilian Transition	16.95	____
____ Jobs and the Military Spouse	17.95	____
____ Military Resumes and Cover Letters	21.95	____
____ Military-to-Civilian Career Transition Guide	15.95	____
____ Military to Federal Career Guide	38.95	____
____ Military Transition to Civilian Success	21.95	____

Ex-Offenders in Transition

____ 9 to 5 Beats Ten to Life	15.00	____
____ 99 Days and a Get Up	9.95	____
____ Best Resumes and Letters for Ex-Offenders	19.95	____
____ Ex-Offender's Job Hunting Guide	17.95	____
____ Ex-Offender's Job Search Companion	11.95	____
____ Ex-Offender's Quick Job Hunting Guide	9.95	____
____ Life Without a Crutch	7.95	____
____ Man, I Need a Job	7.95	____

Changing Addictive and Not-So-Hot Behaviors

____	The Addictive Personality	14.95 ____
____	Angry Men	14.95 ____
____	Angry Women	14.95 ____
____	Denial Is Not a River in Egypt	12.95 ____
____	How to Quit Drugs for Good!	16.95 ____
____	No One Is Unemployable	29.95 ____
____	Passages Through Recovery	14.95 ____
____	Sex, Drugs, Gambling and Chocolate	15.95 ____
____	Stop the Chaos	12.95 ____
____	The Truth About Addiction and Recovery	14.00 ____
____	Understanding the Twelve Steps	12.00 ____
____	You Can Heal Your Life	12.95 ____

Government and Security Jobs

____	Book of U.S. Government Jobs	21.95 ____
____	Complete Guide to Public Employment	19.95 ____
____	Federal Applications That Get Results	23.95 ____
____	FBI Career Guide	15.00 ____
____	FBI Careers	19.95 ____
____	Federal Law Enforcement Careers	19.95 ____
____	Post Office Jobs	19.95 ____
____	Ten Steps to a Federal Job	39.95 ____

International and Travel Jobs

____	Back Door Guide to Short-Term Job Adventures	21.95 ____
____	Big Guide to Living and Working Overseas	49.95 ____
____	Careers in International Affairs	24.95 ____
____	The Global Citizen	16.95 ____
____	Going Global Career Guide	195.95 ____
____	How to Get a Job in Europe	21.95 ____
____	International Jobs	19.00 ____
____	International Job Finder	19.95 ____
____	Jobs for Travel Lovers	19.95 ____
____	Teaching English Abroad	19.95 ____
____	Work Worldwide	14.95 ____
____	Work Your Way Around the World	19.95 ____

VIDEOS/DVDs

Interview, Networking, and Salary

____	Best 10¼ Tips for People With a Not-So-Hot Past	98.00 ____
____	Build a Network for Work and Life	99.00 ____
____	Common Mistakes People Make in Interviews	79.95 ____
____	Exceptional Interviewing Tips	79.00 ____
____	Extraordinary Answers to Interview Questions	79.95 ____
____	Extreme Interview	69.00 ____
____	Make a First Good Impression	129.00 ____
____	Seizing the Job Interview	79.00 ____
____	Quick Salary Negotiations Video	129.00 ____
____	Why Should I Hire You?	99.00 ____

Dress and Image Videos

____	Head to Toe	98.00/108.00 ____
____	Tips & Techniques to Improve Your Total Image	98.00/108.00 ____

Resumes, Applications, and Cover Letter Videos

____	Building the Right Resume and Cover Letter	129.00 ____
____	The Complete Job Application	99.00 ____
____	Quick Cover Letter Video	129.00 ____
____	Quick Resume Video	129.00 ____
____	Resumes, Cover Letters, and Portfolios	98.00 ____

Attitude, Motivation, and Empowerment Videos

____	Down But Not Out	129.00 ____
____	Looking for Work With Attitude Plus	99.00 ____

SUBTOTAL _____

Virginia residents add 5% sales tax _____

POSTAGE/HANDLING ($5 for first product and 8% of SUBTOTAL) __$5.00__

8% of SUBTOTAL ------------------------------------- _____

TOTAL ENCLOSED ----------------------- _____

SHIP TO:

NAME _____

ADDRESS _____

_____

_____

PAYMENT METHOD:

❑ I enclose check/money order for $ _____ made payable to IMPACT PUBLICATIONS.

❑ Please charge $ _____ to my credit card:
❑ Visa ❑ MasterCard ❑ American Express ❑ Discover

Card # _____ Expiration date: ____/____

Signature _____

The Career Savvy Series

Resume, Application, and Letter Tips for People with Hot and Not-So-Hot Backgrounds
185 Tips for Landing the Perfect Job
Ron and Caryl Krannich, Ph.Ds

Each year over 25 million Americans conduct a job search that involves writing resumes and letters and/or completing applications. However, many of these job seekers make numerous writing mistakes that prevent them from landing job interviews. Reflecting the experiences of many job seekers, employers, and career experts, this book outlines 185 tips for creating more effective resumes, letters, and applications. Rich with quizzes, examples, and websites. ISBN 1-57023-240-7. 2006. 224 pages. $17.95

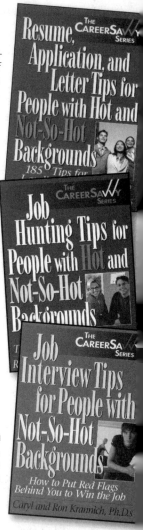

Job Hunting Tips for People With Hot and Not-So-Hot Backgrounds
150 Smart Tips That Can Change Your Life
Ron and Caryl Krannich, Ph.Ds

Finding a job may be the hardest, most frustrating, and ego-bruising work you will ever do. Depending on how you approach the process, it can also be an extremely educational, exciting, and exhilarating experience. This unique book presents 150 job hunting tips that are applicable to most job seekers, regardless of their backgrounds. Organized around a step-by-step job search process, it includes tips on everything from conducting a self-assessment, developing an objective, and conducting research to completing applications, writing resumes and letters, networking, interviewing, and negotiating salary. 2005. 240 pages. ISBN 1-57023-225-3. $17.95

Job Interview Tips for People With Not-So-Hot Backgrounds
Caryl and Ron Krannich, Ph.Ds.

You must do well in the job interview to get a job offer. But what should you say and do if your background includes red flags—you've been incarcerated, got fired, received poor grades, or lack necessary skills? This book speaks to millions of individuals who have difficult but promising backgrounds. Shows how to best prepare for interview questions that could become job knock-outs. Filled with numerous examples and cases to illustrate how to provide honest and positive answers. 2004. ISBN 1-57023-213-X. $14.95.